COMING TO OUR SENSES
Reclaiming the Dignity of Organization Life

Ron Knowles
Western Management Consultants of Ontario

Forbes
CUSTOM PUBLISHING

NEW YORK · CHICAGO · WASHINGTON D.C. · LOS ANGELES · TORONTO

CIP Data is available.
Printed in Canada.
10 9 8 7 6 5 4 3 2 1

ISBN 0–8281–1335–1

ACKNOWLEDGMENTS

I cannot remember whether the idea for this book was mine or my friend and mentor Bob Catherwood's. Bob was a distinguished business journalist before his untimely death. I know my decision to proceed resulted from one of our long lunches when he was doing one of the things he did best—using his genius at inspiring by quiet encouragement and example.

Several of my clients, gifted leaders in their own right, generously made time available to discuss the issues and challenge my thinking. Some are mentioned, others preferred not to be.

My editor Barbara Novak guided me and taught me and was a delight to work with.

My business partners in the Western Management Consultants family provided needed moral and material support as well as their own organizational experience. And my wife Linda, as life partners should, tirelessly encouraged and where necessary cajoled me.

TABLE OF CONTENTS

PART I

STILL SEARCHING FOR EXCELLENCE

CHAPTER 1

COMING TO OUR SENSES

It was the best of times. It was the worst of times.
—Charles Dickens, *A Tale of Two Cities*

This book is directed at people who have leadership roles in organizations. This normally includes chief executive officers, other executives, managers and supervisors. In the modern organization, leadership is remarkably diffuse and includes people whose leadership function might be informal or temporary, such as people involved in special projects or sales and marketing people who coordinate key client relationships. The issues addressed in this book affect anyone in a leadership role, and may also be of interest to people who are interested in leadership or in organization effectiveness, such as consultants or students.

The world of this book is the organization, a place where, like so many others, I have spent my working life. I have never lost my fascination with what people do to organizations and what organizations do to people. In the mid-1990s, despite a successful career and a lifelong affection for and belief in organizations, I found myself reflecting on the value of my working life. Had I devoted whatever talent I may have to a worthwhile purpose? I know a lot of other people ask themselves such disturbing questions. I was in the fortunate position of being able to take a sabbatical to think about what I had learned in my career and what, if anything, my experiences had amounted to. It turned out to be deeply rewarding. I realized that a career spent within organizations trying to make things better is profoundly important and challenging. It's easy to be so distracted by all the imperfections and pressures of organization life that you lose sight of what attracted you in the first place. In my case, it was the opportunity to grow through learning, to build rich relationships and to do some good in the world. On sabbatical, I found myself exploring the gaps between those goals and the reality of day-to-day experience with its endless stream of good and bad, highs and lows, triumphs and disappointments, inspiration and disillusionment. I came to see that the experience we have of organization life cannot be separated from our individual personal world and that the moment we cease trying to make the organization better and more effective is the moment we begin to move backwards. That means we have to strive to understand and create a better working world for ourselves and for others and for the organization as a productive and successful entity.

Organizations are organic creations, either constantly striving for improvement or beginning the process of decline. They could all do more good and less harm, not only to themselves and the people who work for them, but also in the wider worlds in which they operate. Being part of an organization may be delightful or depressing. It is often both. But no one is untouched by the experience.

I don't believe that the way we experience life in an organization depends as much on whether it is in the private, public, or not-for-profit sector as we might like to believe. In some ways these distinctions are important and there are some qualitative differences between sectors. But there are a lot of myths about how much harder people in the private sector work and how much more action-oriented they are. The issues that this book addresses affect organizations of all kinds.

By and large, organizations are good places to be. But not good enough. They bring out the best in us. They also bring out the worst in us. Something happens to even the nicest people when they take on their organizational persona. Our normal human imperfections assume a more odious form. What is it about organizations, for example, that seems to spawn vicious rivalries, or petty despotism, or incipient dishonesty among the normal, conscientious people we meet every day? Why does the interaction of people and organizations so often lead to a strange brew of good and bad which no one intends and everyone agrees is distasteful?

My experience suggests that the frustrating downside of organization life is largely systemic; an unexpected outcome of other, often innocent, factors. Such as the fact that we frequently avoid acknowledging chronic problems that require concerted effort to solve. Or the fact that we don't like to admit that most policies and actions have negative as well as positive consequences. Or that people, being human, are tempted to exploit situations to their own benefit if they can. Or that we tend to see our own motives as highly principled even when they are also self interested. And occasionally—but only occasionally—because someone is consciously trying to do harm to another, or to achieve greater personal advantage at someone else's expense.

IT'S TIME TO COME TO OUR SENSES

Organization life is plagued with serious contradictions. They are well known to anyone who spends time in businesses, government departments or not-for-profit agencies. That includes organization leaders and the people they lead.

The biggest contradiction is the contrast between the fast-moving, customer-centered, efficient organizations which have emerged from the recent era of radical transformation and the human angst and despair which seem almost universal in those same organizations. It can be dangerous to express the dark underside of contemporary organizations. But scratch the surface and you quickly discover widespread stress, alienation and cynicism. This is not an original insight. It is common knowledge, although not always among the senior members of the organization. Organization angst (that chronic, low-grade, emotional down feeling, part depression, part worry that won't go away easily) is devastating, not only in human terms, but also in the effect it has on organization effectiveness. Unfortunately, there are no valid ways of measuring its real impact on organization effectiveness. For this reason, some people still think of "soft" issues as having only secondary importance to performance, a misunderstanding which perpetuates the spiral of growing cynicism, fatigue and indifferent performance which increasingly infects our organizations.

It is time we looked squarely at the many baffling contradictions we encounter in organizations. To continue to ignore them, or to acknowledge them and merely shrug our shoulders is soul destroying, and I am speaking of both human and organizational souls. When we work in a soulless organization, we grow alienated from it, no matter how many team-building workshops we may attend. How can we take our work or our organizations seriously in the face of such fundamental contradictions? To find them, we need only look in the gaps between theory and practice.

On the one hand, we urge leaders to empower people by passing decision authority closer to the "front line." At the same time, we expect our leaders to readily accept full accountability for anything that might go wrong. The theory is that because leaders influence decisions and performance of others through the processes, systems and environments they create, they are the ones to blame when things go wrong. This is a proposition of dubious logic since there are limits to the control leaders can exercise on the actions of others. President Ford argued persuasively that there are real limits to the power of even the *President of the United States*, clearly the most powerful role there is.

The day-to-day experience of people in organizations is rife with the most ludicrous contradictions. For example, although we know that organization politics are a real factor, they are rarely (openly) discussed as a legitimate consideration in decision making. In the field of process improvement, we still expect people to contribute ideas, in full knowledge that their implementation may lead to the replacement of their own work. We all know of the boss who preaches that people should maintain balance in their work/personal life, while frequently assigning urgent tasks which make achieving such balance impossible.

Sustained performance depends on eliminating the contradictions, but we will never succeed until we stop seeking simple solutions. It's tempting to fall into the habit of buying in too easily to the latest theory, or adapting practices that have driven the success of some other company, without considering whether or not they fit our own. The media is filled with stories of how Corporation ABC became the industry leader by adopting a particularly brilliant strategy. *The truth is rarely that simple.* It is simplistic to ascribe brilliance or unusual foresight to organizations in retrospect and sobering to revisit the most admired organizations years later to see how many continue to occupy their positions of leadership and respect. Of course, some organizations do, but many more prove to be paragons only in the media, not in reality. Organizations, like people, fulfill Andy Warhol's prediction with their 15 minutes of fame.

Serious contradictions arise for other reasons as well. We are all guilty of wishful thinking. For example, it is easier to hope that the appointment of an unpopular executive will be supported than to bring someone in from outside. Or to use the fact that the CEO is receiving little negative feedback to convince ourselves that a new organization structure is working well, despite evidence to the contrary. Or we may apply the principle of the pigs in George Orwell's *Animal Farm*, who proclaimed that: "All animals are equal, but some animals are more equal than others." We see that in organizations in which a new values statement is expected to apply more to junior than to senior people.

This book examines these and other reasons why the most serious contradictions occur. The reality is that people see the contradictions much more clearly than leaders seem to believe. And the contradictions and inconsistencies are horribly demotivating. They exact a huge cost in leadership credibility and, over time, build up an impenetrable layer of psychological resistance, a form of dissociation.

Still, there are many positives. Most people have a love/hate relationship with their organization. The contemporary organization is often an exciting

place to be. There is as much to enjoy as there is to deplore. The pace is invig-
orating and the expectations challenging. Co-workers can be a source of
pleasure and meaning. For any individual, the balance of love and hate
depends on a myriad of factors, one of the most important of which is leadership, a key theme of this book.

A HIGH STAKES GAME

In urging that leaders adopt a more independent and self-confident
approach to deciding how their organizations should approach their circumstances, we are involved in a high stakes game. As we all know, working life is
terribly rushed and frenetic. Decisions with far reaching consequences are
made without adequate analysis or reflection. At the same time, we all suffer
from information overload; we are deluged with recipes about how to think or
act. But decisions have to be made in this cauldron of sweeping change, global
competition and burgeoning technology. Bad decisions lead ultimately to
business failure—nobody wins and the costs can be horrendous for investors,
customers, executives and employees. Good decisions depend on good information. This means looking objectively at organization realities. That's why
courageous and honest leadership is more important than ever.

We have the capacity to look at the realities and begin resolving the
contradictions. People at the top of companies, governments and agencies
have the capacity to understand what they see. What they need is the confidence to look with their own eyes not somebody else's.

POISONED ENVIRONMENT FOR LEADERS

Although they have the ability and the primary responsibility to remove
the contradictions of organization life, leaders bear a special burden. Not only
are they expected to resolve for others the soul-destroying inconsistencies, but
they also must live with and overcome the effects of these contradictions on
themselves. It is increasingly fashionable to be critical of our leaders. Unfortunately, a stream of negative examples such as those of President Clinton, to
name only one of far too many examples, have poisoned the atmosphere in
which all leaders must operate.

My own perspective is much more positive. The many CEOs I have met
have been, by and large, good and gifted people who genuinely have the best
interests of their organizations at heart. Most people do not know how difficult it is to be a good leader. I know this because of the mixed results I have
achieved, in spite of my best efforts, in the several leadership roles I have
played in industry, consulting and as a volunteer board member. Even though

this book is a directive to leaders to come to their senses, I have great respect for the enormous challenges leaders face. This book provides constructive advice on how they can develop a more realistic view and approach to organization realities.

I consider myself a veteran of organizational life. During a career spent one half inside organizations as a manager and executive and one half outside as a management consultant, I have worked with hundreds of organizations on issues such as setting strategic direction and facilitating organization change and transformation. Like many of my colleagues, I continue to bump into the same issues and problems, time and time again. Some of them are chronic problems, such as dealing well with low performance, and communicating credibly, particularly familiar issues that are remarkably persistent and intransigent, and therefore increasingly frustrating for all concerned. Other contradictions represent new threats to organization effectiveness, including the misuse of consultation as a management tool and the negative effects of downsizing as a change strategy. Such issues are at the heart of the ennui and dysfunctionality that are sapping the strength and energy of even our most resilient organizations.

This book represents a synthesis of issues and ideas that have been emerging for several years, a synthesis which encompasses those issues which have become the most perplexing and stubbornly resistant to change.

Each of the selected issues is dealt with in a separate chapter which sets out why that problem has developed, why it is so tough to solve and what can be done, practically, to achieve fundamental improvement.

The Present Organization Effectiveness Paradigm: History or Future explores the ideas and biases we have about what makes organizations perform effectively, why that paradigm is getting a little frayed around the edges and the concepts that appear to be replacing it. This chapter is based on my research with a cross section of leaders in almost 100 organizations.

Strategic Planning Isn't focuses on the problems organizations have in trying to make their strategic planning initiatives effective, why strategic planning so often fails to meet objectives and what is necessary for effective planning.

Down with Downsizing challenges leaders to examine the full impact of organization downsizing and asks leaders to consider alternatives to downsizing.

Fairness—Everyone's Core Value examines the place of fairness and equity in our value system, the good and bad implications, and strategies to balance fairness with effectiveness.

Leadership—Character Meets Context analyzes why we are increasingly resistant to our leaders, the implications for people in leadership roles and strategies to lead in the emergent organization.

The Cult of Consultation explores some of the excesses in use of consultation as a leadership technique and how consultation should be understood and practiced by leaders and the people they lead.

Up Front, In Control and Articulate deals with some the leadership skills and role requirements which are not taught in business school, but should be because their absence can single handedly destroy the careers of the even the most gifted people.

Build It and They Will Stay explores the current crisis in balancing all of the demands people face in their working and personal lives. This problem, about which much is said and little done, is reaching epidemic proportions and is already affecting the quality of organization performance.

Caring Enough to Confront—How to Manage Performance and Behaviour Problems deals with the chronic difficulty organizations have in providing performance feedback to people in a way that creates positive change instead of setting up a spiral of declining relationships and deteriorating performance. Strategies for dealing with performance feedback challenges are presented.

Making Organization Change Stick sets out the reasons why, in this time of unprecedented change, organization change efforts so often underachieve their goals, can make things worse, and suggests strategies to improve the prospects of achieving positive, constructive change.

Communicating the Truth, the Whole Truth and Nothing but the Truth is a critique of today's organization communication practices with their emphasis on positive spin and use of jargon, together with strategies by which leaders can communicate more credibly.

Show Me the Money presents a perspective on why the increased attention paid in the media to executive compensation practices has led to a politicization of compensation management and how companies should approach the sensitive issues involved in defining the executive pay package.

REGAINING PERSPECTIVE

There is nothing new about this particular list of problem issues. The management literature is brimming with prescriptions, models and theories that address them. That is part of the problem. We have grown so used to the idea that there is a magic bullet solution for all problems that we tend to substitute the latest fad or somebody else's solution for one based on our own experience and judgment. Only the most confident leaders can resist the temptation to buy the ideas of management gurus, since they seem so authoritative and compelling. But this flies in the face of what we already know: *success comes from applying the right idea in the right context, and implementing well.* This is another theme of this book—that leaders need to keep up to date on emerging management techniques, but never abdicate their responsibility to select and implement the solution that best fits their own circumstances. It takes real confidence to resist conventional wisdom or the latest management fad and to go with your own instincts. This is what I mean by *coming to our senses.* It means taking the time to check out what is really going on in your organization, without wishful thinking, and having the courage to face the facts as they are.

My advice to leaders—executives and managers—is to try to keep up, as best they can, with the growing management literature and with the best practices of other organizations. There is very wise counsel available. The ideas of Henry Mintzberg on planning and management, the recommended approaches to organization change of John Kotter and David Nadler and the provocative approach to leadership advocated by Ron Heifetz are examples of the richness and stimulation to be found in the business bookstore. *But remember that as helpful as outside ideas are, they are never a substitute for the thoughtful analysis and confident decisions of the organization's own leaders.* The trick is to avoid applying recipes developed in some other industry or environment, mindlessly following fads, or going for the pat solutions. The greatest value of the management literature is to help equip leaders to analyze and diagnose what is really happening in their own organizations and to provide ideas about how those circumstances can be successfully addressed.

WHAT PEOPLE ARE REALLY LIKE

This requires that leaders take a less simplistic view of people. We tend to rely on a few highly subjective and wildly exaggerated assumptions about what makes people tick. We think in terms of "good" people and "bad" people. We imagine that good people will always be well intentioned, creative, hard working, open minded, objective and highly principled. We imagine that bad people will always be resistant to change, self interested and lazy. Both views are equally unrealistic. Still, we tend to swing between these two opposing views of people, depending on our own mood and mind set, even though our experience makes it obvious that the same people can be brilliant or useless, lazy or tireless depending on the circumstances. Everyone is, of course, a mixture of good and bad, principled and self interested, responsible and irresponsible. We both delight and frustrate our co-workers. We have good days and bad days. When we are anxious or demoralized, we all are capable of negative behaviour, from pettiness all the way to insubordination and sabotage. Whether we present the mostly positive or mostly negative side of our character depends not only on us, but also whether in our heart of hearts we think that the organization deserves our best efforts. It is also useful to remember that we apply the same demanding standards to our leaders as they do to us. The one thing that is beyond the capacity of any of us is perfection. The fact that we make mistakes is not only inevitable, it is normal.

Finally, we need to stop labeling and start seeking solutions. Once people are perceived as "problems," it is very difficult for them to be seen in any other way. We are forever fulfilling our own prophecies. Perceptions change far less readily than behaviors; once established, a bad reputation is almost impossible to change.

We need to do better than this. Our challenge as leaders is to draw out the good and mitigate the bad. If we accept that a person's behavior results from the interaction between the system and the individual, then we should avoid making sweeping value judgments and instead begin to identify and address the systemic and individual problems that can be solved.

My intention with this book is to present a balanced picture of the good and the bad. Eminent golf teacher Jim McLean tells his students, "I will teach you the eight things in the golf swing you must do and also some things that you absolutely must not do." He doesn't concentrate *only* on the positive. Organization leadership is like that. There are some things that you should do and some things that you should *not* do. Unfortunately, we live in an age where pointing out the problems is thought to be hopelessly negative. The management and leadership literature is filled with prescriptive models and theories—the one right way to lead. It doesn't work that way. Like golf, leadership not only demands good technique, it also depends on the ability to apply techniques to ambiguous and rapidly changing circumstances. Also, like golf, leadership requires the wisdom to avoid the many shoals that lie under the surface. The pat solutions we find all around us are dangerous. They encourage us to oversimplify complex realities. But most importantly, they lead us to lose confidence in our own competence and the value of our own experience. The strategies presented in the following chapters are not intended as pat solutions. Grounded in the reality of organization life, they are intended to be applied thoughtfully; in a way that suits your unique circumstances.

CHAPTER **2**

THE PRESENT ORGANIZATION EFFECTIVENESS PARADIGM: HISTORY OR FUTURE?

This book is a call to come to our senses. Am I suggesting that we have lost our senses? No, but I think that they have been buried under the weight of all the mythology that has built up around our current organization effectiveness paradigm. We rely on "experts" to tell us how to go about things, and persist in that behavior even when, logically, it might not make sense. This is what leads to a loss of dignity, and certainly to a loss of effectiveness. The time has come to examine the reality of our circumstances to find the simple truth; to see what does and does not work.

An organization effectiveness paradigm is the commonly accepted framework of principles, concepts and models that we believe lead to high performing organizations. For almost 20 years, we have been working with an amazingly consistent set of ideas and beliefs about how organizations should be managed. This integrated framework of concepts (or paradigm) first set out in *In Search of Excellence* has achieved a level of acceptance and staying power which is unprecedented.[1] But there are signs that people are growing tired of the rhetoric associated with the ideas, if not the ideas themselves, and that we may be in for a sea change. The paradigm may be losing its usefulness. It has been misapplied and corrupted over time. Our growing frustration may stem from an overfamiliarity with its concepts, or from applying it to situations it does not fit. Too often, we have been swept away by the enthusiasm for the next quick fix and have applied management fads indiscriminately. Or, to

---

[1] *In Search of Excellence*, by Thomas Peters and Robert H. Waterman, Jr. New York: Harper & Ross, 1982.

take a more optimistic view, the paradigm may simply be evolving. In any case, it is no longer working the way it once did, and whether the cause lies with the paradigm itself or with the unthinking way people understand and implement it, it has led to a loss of perspective which badly needs to be redressed.

A major part of the problem lies in our tendency in organization life to misuse perfectly good ideas by discussing them in terms of jargon. In the process, we lose perspective. Sometimes the use of jargon indicates a lack of understanding of the underlying concepts. It may result from the brutal pace of modern day organizational life, a pace that causes us to cut corners by using jargon and to grasp at the latest ideas, no matter how superficially we understand them or how imperfectly they might fit our situation, in the hopes that they will solve the myriad of challenges we face. It is a sad fact that we often destroy the usefulness of the best thinking and insights because we apply them so badly.

The proposition that our organization effectiveness paradigm is reaching the natural end of its life cycle has been tested during the past two years in workshops with management groups and among three groups of MBA students. Judgment as to whether the paradigm is passing or evolving is split, with perhaps slightly more workshop participants holding the view that the underlying organization effectiveness assumptions are evolving. This is an important distinction since it sheds light on the question of whether we should be seeking to apply known ideas more effectively or finding new concepts upon which to base our improvement efforts.

RE-EXAMINING THE CURRENT PARADIGM

The current management paradigm dates from 1982 when Peters and Waterman published their landmark book, *In Search of Excellence*. Many of the key elements were set out there for the first time, including:

- a bias for action
- closeness to the customer
- organization structures which provide more autonomy and entrepreneurship and which are designed to be simpler and leaner
- productivity through people
- hands-on, values-driven leadership
- focus on quality

The book's basic ideas, which won rapid and enthusiastic acceptance, were further developed and modified by academicians and consultants. While we can find tremendous diversity in the particular ways in which they have been applied, the basic ideas remain essentially the same. Today they are virtually universal, providing the foundation for almost every organization change program, even in organizations which have not overtly changed at all. But after more than 20 years and countless applications, the time has come to re-examine these ideas with a critical eye, to see where they have become less effective than they once were, for this will identify the point of evolution for most organizations today. They boil down to six main themes.

1. Explicitly stated purpose and values.

It is the exceptional organization that doesn't have a written statement setting out its fundamental purpose (mission), its direction (vision) and its values. We generally accept that clarifying these fundamental articles of organizational philosophy is a useful exercise for the leaders involved and, more importantly, one that will provide guidance to all employees as they undertake their day-to-day tasks, trade-offs and decisions. Some organizations go to great lengths to communicate their basic values to customers, suppliers and other stakeholders. As discussed in Chapter 9 ("Build It and They Will Stay"), one mission statement has a tendency to sound much like any other and most organizations espouse similar values. In spite of the difficulties of defining a truly distinctive role in the larger scheme of things, people in organizations generally find it helpful to know what the organization values and how it defines its direction. I have, however, noticed a growing impatience in planning workshops. Often they are characterized by intense, highly introspective debates over the precise wording to be used in such statements. As important as clarity is, such a tendency to focus on excessively refining the language used to express every nuance of an organization's mission, vision and values (sometimes called "wordsmithing") suggests a misplaced fussiness. It's as though the leaders imagine if they could just *say* it right, it would happen. But there's more to it than that.

2. Commitment to meeting customer needs and expectations.

One of the most positive aspects of the paradigm has been its intense focus on understanding what customers expect and a dedication to providing it in a way that meets or exceeds expectations. Many organizations try to get out in front of customer expectations and most devote resources to surveying and monitoring both needs and levels of satisfaction.

Deliberately managed programs of customer service improvement have been introduced widely. Many have been highly innovative. A real breakthrough occurred several years ago at a passenger railway company when the president and the vice-presidents adopted the practice of spending one day each quarter working in a front-line customer service role. The then president spent a day collecting tickets during boarding and a regional vice-president worked as a waiter in the club car. At the time, and in that culture, this was regarded as a revolutionary move. Not only did it capture the imagination of the workforce, it also had some substantive benefits. It reminded executives what day-to-day life was like for most of the company's employees.

It is now not so unusual for company executives to participate in programs that bring them more closely into contact with the day-to-day operating environment of customer service. A similar principle is behind the practice of having corporate executives play a personal role in the company's marketing activities by calling on key clients. It is now normal practice for account executives to call on the CEOs and COOs, when new or current business is in the balance.

Many organizations invest heavily in customer service training and communication programs. In telephone customer service operations, technology allows supervisors and other corporate staff to monitor interaction between customers and customer service representatives. One imaginative company loaned its customer service management staff to a major retailer to masquerade as mystery shoppers. The loaned staff completed extensive reports on how well staff had met the established standards in such areas as customer acknowledgment, suggestion selling and responsiveness. And not only were their reports useful to the retailer, but the opportunity to look at service through the customer's eyes proved to be of great benefit to the loaned staff as well.

Some service organizations have combined the concepts of quality and customer service with quality customer service programs. This is natural in cases where the organization's product consists of a service, and how customers perceive its quality is a competitive issue of great importance.

People at any level of an organization with experience in face-to-face customer service realize how demanding and challenging it can be to satisfy clients and customers. The fact is that some people are almost impossible to please. Even the best trained service provider can run into unpleasant situations that occasionally include abuse and threats. Front line customer service staff who live day to day with these realities may have scant respect for the leaders of an organization who do not appear to understand the challenges they face.

The question of who defines good service is a tricky one. The level of customer satisfaction an organization achieves at any point in time depends on the relationship between customer expectations and perceptions of service received. In absolute terms, excellent service doesn't necessarily lead to high customer satisfaction if customers expect something different than they are receiving. Customer service expectations seem to rise continuously, making them ever more challenging to meet. In this tyranny of customer service, employees may feel their problems are not well understood or they are not receiving the support required.

While the virtual explosion in customer service has been good for customers and organizations both, it has raised some challenges that will become increasingly difficult to meet as expectations rise while staff resources continue to be carefully rationed.

3. Purposeful programs of improvement.

Several methodologies have emerged that are designed to help organizations become better and better at what they do. In our firm, we refer to the predominant techniques of improvement as the "unholy trinity" consisting of business process re-engineering, total quality management and continuous improvement. While the tools, terms and approaches of each of these methodologies differ somewhat, they share the common purpose of engaging the organization in a process of identifying opportunities for improvement, involving people at all levels in a search for constructive change, and monitoring success at raising the standard of performance. These improvement methodologies account for much of the jargon developed over the past 15 years, as well as a good share of the skepticism about the value of the latest flavor of the month.

Introducing any improvement strategy involves an element of risk and considerable time before the investment shows any sign of paying off. There are many steps (and potential pitfalls) along the way. Consider the case of one Crown Corporation that was developing plans to introduce a continuous improvement strategy. It quickly became apparent that the teams which had been structured to implement the strategy required significant education in the underlying concepts and how to apply them. In addition, the teams underwent team-building training sessions in order to enable them to work effectively in roles which were quite different from their day-to-day tasks. It was also decided that all employees, whether involved in the early stages of the process or not, should receive extensive communication about the continuous improvement strategy and the implementation plan. Once the teams had completed their training, they began to plan their respective strategies. These preparatory steps, all necessary, took about six months to accomplish before any substantive work could begin on the goal of improving processes. The teams, on average, took another five months to develop their proposed improvements, which were then studied and ultimately approved by the steering committee. The organization had invested very heavily in time, support and consulting services before any positive results were achieved. This took longer than had originally been expected; too long, in fact, to meet the high expectations which had been created.

The reality is that the best known improvement strategies, such as total quality and business process reengineering, require a significant investment in *getting ready* to get started. In balance, however, most organizations would acknowledge positive results and some would claim major positive break-throughs.

4. Working through people.

Most organizations are making sincere efforts to involve employees directly in the development of ideas that will contribute to organizational effectiveness and performance. The three most common methods used to enlist the insights of employees are:

- decentralizing or "devolving" responsibility in order to empower the people who are in the best position to apply it
- adopting more open and consultative forms of communication and management
- using teams to plan and execute key functions

While some people might doubt it, senior management's commitment to a more egalitarian concept of staff relations has been genuine. Whether or not concepts like devolvement and empowerment will survive the inevitable changes in fashion that afflict management thinking remains to be seen, although I certainly hope they will. I have observed real improvement in the results achieved from inclusive approaches to people management. It does much to create buy-in; but this on its own is a relatively limited motivation for working through people. When part of an integrated strategy of building the capacity of the organization to perform and adapt, working through people can enhance the organization in every way.

5. Streamlined organization structures.

On paper, organizations now look very different from how they looked 20 years ago. Typically, we see fewer levels of structure from top to bottom, wider spans of management (with more people reporting directly to each manager) and smaller head offices. Other changes cannot be seen on paper, most notably the emerging concept of the roles of managers as leaders, facilitators, integrators, mentors and resource acquirers.

These changes have been driven partly by the need to cut organization costs and partly by the need to eliminate the stultifying effect that excessive bureaucracy was having on employees. The new organization is a busy place, but it is undoubtedly a more productive place. Most observers would agree that organizations are generally more efficient and resilient. At the same time, business journalists and consultants are observing that organizations have possibly cut back too far (see Chapter 12 for a discussion of the "lack of slack").

6. Accessible, hands-on leadership.

The prevailing paradigm places value on quite a different style of leadership; one characterized by leading from a clear vision and strong principles and accepting the role of integrator of the resources and efforts of all employees.

Some of the familiar terms used to describe this new style of management, such as "management by walking around," characterize it as a far more accessible and active form of leadership. Relationships between management and employees are less formal. Leaders are more likely, for example, to ask to be called by their first names. When speaking to internal groups, they are careful to be complimentary, encouraging and respectful. The style is really very different in this respect and is, for the most part, quite sincere. But the corollary is that such exposure leaves leaders open to hostile questions and very sharp, sometimes hostile personal challenges for which they may not be prepared. And of course, in a large organization, hands-on leadership simply isn't sustainable.

HAS THE CURRENT PARADIGM IMPROVED ORGANIZATIONAL PERFORMANCE?

There is no question that the building blocks which comprise the current paradigm have helped organizations survive the great downturn of the early 1990s. In fact, they are the means by which some managed to cope. The paradigm succeeded in elevating the importance of people on the organizational agenda, and made it possible for customers to assume their rightful place as the *raison d'être* not only of businesses but of governments and not-for-profit organizations as well. In most organizations, the faster pace and sense of purpose is tangible. There has been greater consensus around this set of management ideas than any which preceded it, and it has, in balance, led to improvement.

But in spite of its power, the paradigm appears to be running out of steam. It is now saddled with annoying jargon that undermines the value of the underlying ideas. People are weary of the same old words and the same old ideas, which now seem stale and empty, and they're looking for something fresh and more interesting.

More importantly, the ways in which the paradigm has been defined and applied have given rise to fundamental contradictions that lead to skepticism and anger. For example, some people complain that organizations have become heartless, taking more from people than they have given in return. Almost everyone can cite an example of employees who offered innovative suggestions which, when implemented, have led to job loss, sometimes their own. While organizational performance has increased dramatically, employees and managers have not necessarily benefited economically, particularly in the public and not-for-profit sectors which continue to struggle with tougher and tougher financial constraints. In other instances, people have experienced the paradigm as something intensely focused on process, which may or may not have led to improved results. People have grown cynical and resistant to more of the same, particularly because they feel so stressed and pressured by the increased workload. To everything there is a season.

LOOKING INTO THE CRYSTAL BALL—PATHWAYS OF EVOLUTION

This is certainly one of the most exciting times to be in a corporate leadership position. No one can say for sure how the existing paradigm will change but we are all part of the search team. The new management framework, which is already evolving out of the current one, will depend on honesty, integrity, accountability and a much more seamless integration of individual, customer and corporate needs. New thinking and solutions will need to focus in particular on components that (1) stimulate more innovation, (2) are customer driven, (3) facilitate the transition from the world of employment to the world of work, (4) find means of improving processes, (5) balance individual and group roles and (6) emphasize the integration role of leaders.

1. Stimulate more innovation.

The ability to be innovative will be the key success factor and the only way companies will be able to prosper in the global economy. For most organizations, this will require a big improvement. Organizations will have to supplement the generally good results they have received from team innovation with other sources of innovation. The ability to remain at the forefront of any business will require more effort to stay abreast of developments in other countries and in other industries. It will also require the ability to build further alliances and partnerships.

2. Be customer driven.

We may be merely at the threshold of the consumer revolution. Today's technology-hyped customer will demand an unending flow of new, easy-to-use products and services, and will move on to other suppliers if companies disappoint them. As much as organizations want to invest in creating customer expectations that they can meet, there will be real limits to how much customers can be influenced to accept *any* limitations on what they want and when they want it. The implications are truly daunting. It goes well beyond the relatively simple matter of satisfying customers, to the creation of customer-driven organizations. Various means will be found to bring customers inside to participate in decisions that affect them. Establishing customer advisory councils or conducting customer research is just the beginning. We will see organizations really bringing customers inside, into product design, decision making about customer service policies, and other ways that narrow the boundaries between service provider and customers.

3. Facilitate the transition from the world of employment to the world of work.

Organizations will need to become adept at managing within a broader assortment of employment relationships. These will range from conventional employment to highly flexible and temporary connections. Managing the variety of employees and "near" employees will require new techniques and approaches and the result will be more flexible, more dynamic and more interesting organizations where people with different skills come and go. The framework of employment legislation, common law, labor relations and employee benefits is built on an outdated employment model. In order to accommodate the new labor market realities, it will need to undergo a fundamental change. It will become routine to work with people who look different, sound different, and whose ideas are unusual. Teams will be made up of people who are in for the duration and those who come in, make their contribution and move on. Most organizations can certainly use more variety in perspective and points of view, and will also benefit from the variety of ways of working and styles of communication. When the new organization needs more insight about how some group in society thinks, they may find it easier and faster to invite people in to engage in dialogue rather than conduct a formal market survey. Working with people whose connection to the organization is temporary will certainly be more interesting than hearing the same views from the same people with whom one has been working for years.

4. **Use more efficient processes and improve processes more efficiently.**

While systems and processes will always be important, less staff time will be available for process, as distinct from activities associated directly with providing the services of the organization. It will not be possible to support interminable meetings to discuss and plan every issue. More efficient forms of business process reengineering, for example, will be essential if that methodology is to survive. In the case of process improvement work, it will be important to find methods that take advantage of the knowledge of the people who do the work while avoiding the need to place on their shoulders the entire burden of designing the improvements. New ways of combining the efforts of workers and process improvement specialists will be required.

5. **Balance individual and group roles.**

Organizations will clarify the conditions under which individual accountability is more appropriate than group or team accountability and vice versa. Some tasks are best delegated to the most talented individual, while others require the diversity of perspective and energy that teams can bring.

The highly respected U.K. management theorist, Elliot Jacques, may have single-handedly pushed the pendulum back in the direction of a more traditional understanding of the nature of accountability in his book *Requisite Organization*.[2] He argues that all organizations are, by nature, hierarchically stratified in the sense that a manager is held accountable not only for his/her personal effectiveness but also for the outputs of immediate subordinates. Not surprisingly, *Requisite Organization* has been quite controversial since it emphasizes the importance of accountability, authority and responsibility of managers in relation to their subordinates, suggesting a return, at least on the surface, to the command and control concept of organization structure.

---

[2] *Requisite Organization*, by Elliot Jacques, Cason Hall & Co., Arlington, Virginia, 1989.

Whether *Requisite Organization* represents the creation of a new balance in organization design thinking or not, the book has attracted enormous interest and may make discussing concepts like hierarchy and authority more respectable. Jacques' greatest contribution is to remind us that there is more than one way to approach things and that leadership means employing the right strategy for the right circumstances.

6. Emphasize the integration role of leaders.

Our image of the CEO as the decisive, brilliant strategist is a little simplistic—many decisions are made by a management team or are already decided by the time they reach the top of the pyramid. On the other hand, the CEO probably has more access to information about trends, developments, issues, technologies, both inside and in the external environment, than anyone else. Increasingly, our model of leadership will position the leader to act as a link between people, organizations and issues. In so doing, he or she will shape the overall direction of the organization. A key part of leaders' emerging role will be how to integrate a widening variety of markets, stakeholders, business partners and employee expectations.

STRATEGIES TO ADJUST TO THE CHANGING PARADIGM

1. Keep the best of the older ideas and prepare for the new.

Keeping the best and discarding the rest will be the most reasonable approach for most organizations. Continue to develop and build upon those themes which are likely to be permanent additions to the management tool kit. These include, for example, focus on customer satisfaction, working through people, and more accessible leadership. Others, such as the move to structured improvement methodologies, must be simplified or applied more selectively. In the area of organization change processes, teams and projects which have lost their relevance or are not yielding results should be discontinued or refocused.

The practice of consulting with stakeholders on issues affecting them is likely to be one of the more long-lasting features of the present paradigm. Leaders cannot expect to return to a more black box approach to decision making without disillusioning their followers. This is one Pandora's Box that will not be closed, as long as fostering innovation and achieving buy-in to management initiatives are important considerations. A consultative approach has become a fundamental value in itself. A less inclusive approach would be confusing and deeply resented. The challenge is to learn how to use consultation. The same is true of the focus on customer service and satisfaction. It is very unlikely that customers will accept less than they are currently receiving. In fact, it seems apparent they will continue to demand more. Here the real question is whether the constantly increasing customer expectation will lead to a kind of customer service tyranny in which the relationship between supplier and customer is so one sided that customers seem like enemies. Here again, it is difficult to imagine that the expectations, once developed, can easily be constrained. The place to begin is to examine your own organization to determine which ideas are still valid and which are in need of change.

2. **Reduce the proportion of time devoted to process.**

    This can be achieved by defining the role of task teams more clearly. Avoid involving them in time-consuming information gathering or analysis. Instead, rely on them more as advisors and decision makers. In cases where individuals have expertise, teams should be used sparingly. The tendency to discount the expertise of people with whom you work closely is a very human, but misguided, tendency. Most organizations have ready access to information and expert advice through their networks of industry associations and consultants who know the organization well. Internal or external experts can do a great deal to increase the efficiency of even the most consultative form of decision making by developing position papers or providing information briefings to help bring those who will make the decision up to speed. While task forces and teams certainly have their place, their time should not be wasted on preparatory work that can be done by a few informed people.

3. **Ensure that the organization is taking a balanced short- and long-term perspective.**

    Statements of organization values rarely focus enough on the future. Value statements should include reference to longer-term implications of today's decisions. The importance of investing in the organization's capacity to grow and prosper in the future should be made an explicit part of strategy. Excessive focus on the short-term is clearly dangerous and effective leadership depends on a more balanced perspective.

4. **Plan human resources innovatively.**

    The fundamental question that must be addressed is how to sustain a skilled, competitively superior workforce. It's one thing to talk about human resources as a strategic resource, and quite another to do something useful about it. Investing in human and intellectual capital requires resources, time and patience. It involves more than helping people develop; it requires the introduction of innovative ways of working and more flexible working arrangements. This requires the knowledge and skill of people trained in this field. Human resources planning is an established discipline in some organizations, but not all.

5. **Foster innovation.**

Anticipate a real breakthrough in the amount of effort that will go into promoting innovative thinking. It may become the key leadership priority, both in terms of organizations and people. The tried and true methods of innovation fall into three main categories:

- research and development-oriented activities, ranging from pure research to licensing arrangements and alliances with technology partners
- planning initiatives, in which the requirements for future success are identified
- creative processes, such as brainstorming, which seek to nurture creative thinking and innovation

Investments in research and development and planning initiatives tend to suffer during periods of economic downturn. Internally generated creativity, though essential, is rarely sufficient to access the information and ideas needed for future success. We can expect considerable emphasis on how to be more innovative. It is likely that organizations will use a multi-dimensional approach to generating new knowledge and technology which will lead to new products and services. In addition to generating innovations from within, organizations will look further afield for technology partners they wish to grow with. We can expect to see greater interest in forming relationships with scientists and academicians from anywhere in the world, as well as a continuation of the trend for organizations to devote more time to building relationships with similar organizations in other countries. This external search for innovation will likely consist of an energetic blending of several internal and external techniques, all directed at gaining a competitive edge through innovation.

THE CHANGING PARADIGM

In the workshops we have led at Western Management Consultants on the role of the paradigm, people have shown strong attachment to its organization effectiveness ideas. It is not clear whether their attachment reflected their comfort with the familiar or whether, as one participant put it, "we have never really implemented the current paradigm." The question of whether the paradigm is passing or evolving is a moot point since, in either case, it is clearly changing. The challenge is to identify what to drop and what to add, so that its ideas and principles continue to have the ability to inspire and change our organizational lives for the better. An equally large challenge lies in how we *apply* the concepts that underlie the current and evolving paradigm. As leaders, we need to keep a clear perspective. We need always to be conscious of the underlying ideas which shape our decisions, and to be aware of the dangers of applying them thoughtlessly.

"Coming to our senses" means keeping things in perspective and realizing that the principles and models we use are not magic bullets. Using them effectively and ethically means thinking clearly about how to apply them, not in theory but in the real life of the organization. It also means avoiding excessive jargon and moving to a more direct and straightforward style of communication, based in turn on a more realistic understanding of the nature of people and what they need to contribute wholeheartedly to organizational goals. Each of the remaining chapters focuses on a significant issue that results from the out of kilter way in which the paradigm is currently applied, and identifies what we need to do to come to our senses.

CHAPTER **3**

STRATEGIC PLANNING ISN'T

There's a lot of indifferent strategic planning done these days, and that is reflected in the limited value placed on it. In some ways, there has never been more attention paid to strategizing and visioning and strategic planning. Almost every report or proposal you pick up lays out the strategy which is proposed to address its particular issue. Planning and visioning workshops occur with greater frequency in business and non-business organizations and I seem to spend most weeks and many weekends in workshops designed to help clarify an organization's future vision and strategic direction. On the other hand, time pressure created by downsized organizations is pushing planning off the agenda in a way many feel is quite dangerous, given the need to keep up with the changing environment. What little planning is done tends to be characterized by weariness and a lack of enthusiasm.

One of the most serious shortcomings of strategic planning is that it is not very innovative. We tend to see the same ideas at work no matter where we go. Genuinely creative ideas rarely emerge, and those that do are rarely embraced. Professor Henry Mintzberg of McGill University distinguishes between strategic planning and strategic thinking. He makes a persuasive case that trying to institutionalize thinking in the form of planning processes can not really be done successfully.[1] The same distinction could also apply to visioning. We need visionary thinking as much if not more than we need vision statements. Most strategic planning initiatives focus on creating the outcome in the form of a written statement of vision. Ironically, this puts an end to a creative process which should be ongoing. In order to remain open to present and future possibilities, we must foster innovative thinking on a continual basis.

---

[1] "Musings on Management," by Henry Mintzberg, *Harvard Business Review,* July/August 1996.

The intention is to provide high quality strategic planning and visioning. But if we're going to pay more than lip service to that intention, we need to address five main roadblocks.

1. Crisis management.

When an important customer requires a response, the only option is to provide it. When a key employee threatens to resign, a union to go on strike, a business partner to sue, a banker to withdraw support, or any number of other unexpected crises arise, we have no choice but to respond immediately. Anyone who spends time in organizations is well aware of how much energy is spent dealing with today's crises. And every crisis drives planning off the agenda.

But there are also more subtle reasons why executives seem to spend so much of their time in crisis management. They may find it more comfortable to spend time at what they know best and are good at. There is something inherently satisfying about responding to a problem which requires urgent attention and dealing with it successfully. Far more satisfying than guessing at the distant future, which is what strategic planning seems to require. Some organizations fail to address longer-term or stubborn problems because they seem less interesting or because executives incorrectly assume they are already being addressed. Some initiatives, such as quality, information technology planning and training, are talked about more than acted on, partly because it seems that, no matter how hard you work on them, you can never completely solve them.

Whatever the causes of crisis management, it invariably results in an intolerable drain on resources as key people are diverted from their planned activities to deal with the crisis of the moment. The larger costs come from lost opportunities, as organizations fail to come to grips with key strategic issues.

2. Planning requires a crystal ball.

When people use the term "strategic," they usually mean matters of fundamental importance affecting the future success of the whole organization. All strategy rests on assumptions about future conditions. It's not that the assumptions and predictions will necessarily be inaccurate, it is that they can be completely wrong. We all know this. The longer the time horizon involved in strategic planning, the more uncertain the predictions about the future.

At the same time, we have boundless faith in strategic planning, believing that organizations are much better off with a strategic plan which serves as a focus of shorter-range planning, decision making and resource allocation. Developing a sense of unified direction throughout the organization is vitally important. And we have great faith in the ability of strategic planning to provide that sense of unified direction.

And so we approach planning with conflicting feelings: complete faith in its importance to our future success, and frustration because we know, in spite of our best efforts, we cannot fully predict the environment in which we will be operating in the future. The forces which will shape an organization's environment and markets seem to develop with breathtaking rapidity. We know, for example, that the information technology we'll be using in five years will be much more advanced, but *how* advanced? This is one of the many vital issues that will affect the future success of an organization.

The borderline between an organization's information technology and its business is growing increasingly difficult to define. Is an automatic teller machine information technology or is it banking? Market trends and fashions develop quickly, without any apparent pattern. Will people shop by Internet, or will they still flock to the malls? Corporate takeover and merger activity are also susceptible to booms or busts. The great splurge in leverage buyouts, mergers and acquisitions of the late '80s and the accompanying excesses seem forgotten as we are poised to enter a new period of such activity. The popular television show, *Traders*, romanticizes a dog-eat-dog world of rapacious aggressiveness. Funding cutbacks in the government and not-for-profit sectors are leading to fundamental transformation in those sectors, with long- term effects that can barely be glimpsed.

Because the future is unknowable, we approach long-term planning with trepidation. Executives know they must do their best to prepare organizations for the future but they also know they will be dealing with forces they cannot control and to which they will be hard pressed to adapt. Hence, the love/hate feelings about longer-range planning. We recognize that a clear sense of direction offers considerable benefits, but the picture remains elusive. People who present a clear picture of the future, especially when it is based on demographic evidence, receive high mark for prescience. The trouble is, we eagerly read their predictions as facts, forgetting that no one can see the future clearly. The best planners know that planning involves doing your best to anticipate the future so that you can prepare for it, while recognizing that the future state is something dynamic and changeable, so that all efforts to prepare for it must be subject to continual refinement.

3. Planning is hard to do well.

Good planning requires innovation. True innovation results from hard, slogging, painstaking work. The problem is, no one has the time. For example, very little strategic analysis is done any more and people rely instead on their own industry knowledge to fill in the gaps. Consequently, the people involved may be unaware of important variables or issues that will affect the future. Strategic planning facilitators have long been aware that it is important to keep the process as pragmatic and concrete as possible. People quickly lose patience with abstractions and things that *might* be, particularly if they are as time and work pressured as most of us are. But nevertheless, we need to know about our environment. Without information and knowledge, the value of the vision and plans will be limited and the prospects of innovation remote.

Of the many strategic planning methodologies, one of the most common is SWOT analysis, in which organizations define their strengths, weaknesses, opportunities and threats. The degree of analytical rigor brought to SWOT analysis can vary a great deal, ranging from that conducted by a group of people over a few hours, to that which results in dozens of pages of carefully prepared quantitative and qualitative information. Another classical model requires the identification of key strategic issues, sometimes called driving forces, which must be addressed effectively in order to position the organization for future success. Typically, five to seven such issues are extracted from a review of the organization's environment and circumstances. The selected issues are assigned to teams or departments for management.

Various forms of visioning have emerged in recent years and are now widely used. In visioning, the task is to define what the organization wishes to be at some specified future point, typically three to five years. The vision may be defined in specific details (*e.g.* $450,000,000 of revenue, 1,500 employees, all major North American markets, 5 new major products, etc.) or in general terms (a market image of being the high-quality service provider). The visioning phase is often followed by a comparison stage, in which the desired position described in the vision is compared with the current reality. Then the gaps can be redefined in terms of strategic objectives and used as a basis for detailed planning.

Any of these planning approaches can be used in combination, with some creative and highly unusual results. I once participated in a computer-facilitated planning process which purported to develop a strategic plan for the whole organization in a single working day. The exercise was great fun and useful to the degree that it provided a starting point, but the complexity of a modern organization cannot be reduced to a few hours of casual brainstorming.

Most executives and managers have experienced different kinds of planning processes, both at work and through their not-for-profit involvements. Some have grown cynical of the process because they overestimated their benefits. But periodic attention to the future needs and direction of an organization is too important to be ignored.

4. Closure on a strategic direction or vision excludes other possibilities.

Most strategic planning exercises are organized in such a way that the planners must chose from an assortment of future possible directions. This is why one of my colleagues defines strategic planning as "the making of informed choices." Since the world rarely unfolds the way we expect, committing the organization's resources to a single vision of the future is risky business. So we hedge our bets and implement the adopted strategic plan tentatively, with less energy and singular commitment than is required.

5. Poor implementation.

Everyone is sadly familiar with the elegant strategic plan that ends up gathering dust on the bookshelf. Strategic plans have earned the reputation of being interesting but not particularly useful. It's as if the effort devoted to creating the strategic plan is so great that once it has been accomplished, everyone loses interest, believing that the plan will somehow implement itself.

While conducting an organization review for a client organization recently, I was asked to look at its strategic plan. The document was an excellent piece of work which elegantly set out a set of goals and priorities for five years. These were the precise issues which I knew to be relevant to that organization's future success. Because I have run into this situation so frequently, I was not surprised to discover that almost no one in that organization even knew of the plan's existence. What a waste of countless hours of effort, many of them spent away from families on weekends.

Follow-up is another common problem area, one that arises from a sense that strategic planning is distinct from the real business of the organization. Progress reviews and other means of monitoring progress must be integrated with the normal operational review routines, so that implementation of strategic planning is a regular and accepted part of operations.

STRATEGIES FOR IMPROVING THE EFFECTIVENESS OF STRATEGIC PLANNING

1. Create a "rolling" vision.

It is unlikely that any vision will be realized in every particular. The point is not to create an absolutely correct vision, but to continually refine the existing vision so that it can be adapted to changing circumstances. A vision should represent the organization's best potential, assuming that its plans have been reasonably successful. As long as that is understood, people can readily accept that the vision needs to be revisited on an ongoing basis. No one expects the world to stand still, so it should come as no surprise that thinking which seems visionary today may look dated tomorrow. If people expect the vision to evolve over time, they will be more prepared to participate in keeping it fresh and up to date. Vision is a dynamic concept that requires constant crafting. Its greatest value is to provide a unified sense of direction and a basis for making decisions. That is worth contributing time to, without expecting that the task of planning will ever be finished.

I was recently working with a not-for-profit organization serving a variety of health and social needs of seniors. We were updating their strategic plan. One of our first steps was to examine the mission statement which had been in place for about two years. We began by asking whether the statement was still relevant. This led to a productive discussion resulting in some small modifications and expansions in the statement. The discussion was satisfying on two levels. First, there was general pleasure in being able to validate the judgment of the original architects of the mission statement, even after two years of the most tumultuous growth and change. Second, the relatively minor modifications gave the board the sense that they were involved in a dynamic process of development that served to keep the organization aligned with its changing environment. The board then turned its attention to examining the future vision of the organization in the light of the updated mission statement. This is something one sees more of all the time—the concurrent use of missions and vision statements. The mission defines purpose and the vision direction; the two techniques seem to work very well together.

When creating statements of vision and mission, it is easy to fall into the trap of looking for slogans or catch phrases. The elegance of the best slogans is seductive. Planning teams can spend countless hours searching for the perfect phrase. Ford's slogan "Quality is Job One," Nike's "Just Do It," or, GE's "Progress is Our Most Important Product" all have the capacity to capture the imagination. But a focus on wordsmithing can deflect attention from where it belongs. The best planning defines a clear future direction that unifies people and provides guidance on what is most important. It helps in the process of allocating resources, setting priorities and informing the shorter-term operational planning. Those are its major values and, provided that they are periodically reviewed and updated, strategic plans and their cousins, mission and vision statements, can do those jobs well.

2. Foster innovation.

Strategic planning is an investment in generating the ideas and knowledge which will shape the organization's ongoing development. Not all will come from within the current organization, although it is to be hoped that some will. Strategic thinking means opening the mind to the best ideas regardless of where they come from. Internal brainstorming is a powerful technique to foster creative thinking, but organizations can't afford to limit themselves to their own creativity. Organizations need to expand their intellectual horizons by devoting time and resources to accessing avenues of intellectual inspiration. Forums which bring leading thinkers, including people from other countries, universities and organizations, into the planning process to share their ideas and knowledge had gone out of favor. They are coming back and that's a good thing.

Henry Mintzberg maintains that great strategists are either creative or generous and we have too few of either type. We call the creative ones "visionaries"—they see a world to which others are blind. They can be difficult people, but they break new ground. The generous ones bring strategy out in other people. They build organizations that foster thoughtful inquiry and creative action and they strengthen the whole circle by turning strategic thinking into a collective learning process.[2]

We need to avoid bureaucratizing the planning process. This occurs when we restrict thinking and innovation to a specific step in planning. For example, benchmarking has a role in an innovation generation process, but not the only role. It deals more with what has already been done successfully and less with what is being thought and talked about. Organizations must demonstrate that they value fresh thinking and are prepared to devote time and energy, not only to being open minded, but also to seeking knowledge from outside.

3. Eliminate planning duplication.

Prior to the early '90s recession, the organization charts of many businesses included a chief planning officer whose duties included short- and long-range planning, mergers and acquisitions and fostering innovation. Many of these departments have disappeared, partly for economic reasons and partly because of the growing belief that institutionalizing strategic planning reduces the quality of strategic thinking. Now that planning is recognized as an integral part of every manager's job, there is some reluctance to centralize it

---

[2] "Musings on Management," by Henry Mintzberg, *Harvard Business Review,* July/August 1996.

in a single organization unit. We can't know for sure whether eliminating planning departments has increased or decreased the quality of planning activities, particularly since planning is so frequently pushed off the agenda by today's crises and work pressures.

Strategic and visionary thinking are everyone's responsibility. But every organization would benefit from a unified focal point for planning and innovation. Certainly those organizations which are least prepared for the future would benefit from a return to planning departments. But whether an organization's strategic planning is funneled through a department or a focal point, in order for it to be effective the thinking must be *integrative*. It needs to be linked to what is already known throughout the whole organization. I have encountered too many organizations with multiple (and sometimes conflicting) mission statements, simply because the processes which produced them involved different people and had not been integrated. That results in a situation described best by Canadian economist and humorist Stephen Leacock, whose hero, Lord Ronald, "flung himself from the room, flung himself upon his horse and rode madly off in all directions."[3]

4. Balance planning and implementation planning.

At most strategic planning workshops, implementation planning receives a fraction of the time and energy given to creating the direction itself. It is discussed at the end, when people are tired and anxious to leave. It may be delegated to a few people in a way which underscores its relative lack of importance. Invariably, if the plan ends up on the shelf, the breakdown can be traced to poor implementation planning.

Implementation planning involves the definition of tasks, assignment of responsibility and scheduling. Since most organizations are skilled at these activities, there's no reason why the quality of implementation planning should be so poor. If strategic planning and implementation planning are structured as two distinct and equally important phases of the planning process, implementation is more likely to receive the focused attention it requires. Another strategy is to specify what individual managers and leaders need to do personally to implement the plan, and if this can be directly tied to compensation, all the better.

---

[3] "Gertrude the Governess or Simple Seventeen," by Stephen Leacock, originally published in 1911 and reprinted in *The Great Big Book of Canadian Humour*, edited by Allan Gould, Macmillan Company, 1992, p. 173.

Successful implementation is a matter of leadership and discipline. Unless an organization is committed to implementing its strategic plans, those plans become nothing more than academic exercises. Who's got the time or the inclination to navel gaze at the future? It's not enough just to think about it, or even to talk about it. The final stage of strategic planning is to do something to actualize the vision of the future, to make that vision a reality.

CHAPTER 4

DOWN WITH DOWNSIZING

In any discussion of the advisability of downsizing, a distinction needs to be made between terminating the services of a individual person because of his or her inability to sustain adequate levels of performance or appropriate behavior, and those whose services the organization can no longer afford. In the case of low performing employees or those with unproductive attitudes and behavior, termination may be the only solution, particularly if concerted attempts have been made to help the employee address the problem areas, as discussed in Chapter 10.

This chapter reflects on the other reasons for downsizing. In the early 1980s organizations seemed to be caught up in a kind of frenzy of firing veteran staff. At that time I published an article entitled "Executive Firing Has Gone a Step Too Far" which expressed my concern about the human and organization costs of that growing practice.[1] I cautioned that organizations were divesting themselves of the very people who had helped build them and who possessed most of the background knowledge and historical perspective needed for balanced decision making. Further, I wondered about the effect on the children of fired executives. Would witnessing their parents' pain cause them to avoid business as a future career choice?

That was 1983 and I was witnessing only the tip of the iceberg. In the intervening decade and a half, the pace of organizational downsizing and accompanying job loss has increased dramatically. It is difficult to find reliable figures on how much job loss has occurred but it is certain that tens of thousands of management people were fired during that period.

Henry Mintzberg reflected on this in the *Harvard Business Review*. "There is nothing wonderful about firing people," he observed. "True, stock market

---

[1] "Executive Firing Has Gone a Step Too Far," by Ron Knowles, *Financial Post*, 1983.

analysts seem to love companies that fire front-line workers and middle managers (while increasing the salaries of senior executives). Implicitly, employees are blamed for having been hired in the first place and are sentenced to suffer the consequences while the corporations cash in." The irony of the situation is abundantly clear, as well as his impatience with it. "Lean is *mean*. So why do we keep treating people in these ways? Presumably because we are not competitive. And just why aren't we competitive? To a large extent, because we have been unable to meet Japanese competition. So how do we respond? By managing in exactly the opposite way than the Japanese. Will we never learn?"[2]

But so far Mintzberg is in the minority. Few people have questioned the wisdom of trying to improve the bottom line by significantly reducing the workforce. Corporate CEOs demonstrated to their boards and investors that they had "the right stuff," the inner toughness required to fire people. And what happened to all of the middle-aged middle managers who have been let go? The large re-employment counseling firms keep careful track of how long it takes their clients to find alternate employment. Generally, managers who have been fired are finding alternative employment, but of a significantly different nature. Many are finding work as contract employees, consultants or project managers. Fewer are finding traditional employment in larger organizations. And sadly, some never reconnect at all. They drop off into non-employment or early retirement for which they may be financially and personally unprepared. While the impact of job loss on individuals and their families can be horrendous, it's not clear that we care all that much as a society. The plight of the unemployed is just one of a myriad of issues which crowd the social agenda. The situation of the managerial unemployed seems to find no organized expression through lobbies or activist groups.

We have honed the art of firing people to a high level. Many organizations have established relationships with re-employment counselors to whom they can delegate responsibility to help, for a fee, the people they have shed. The rules by which severance payments and out-of-court settlements are reached are well understood and can be managed efficiently. The techniques of firing, now highly developed, can be readily applied by any organization. Aside from the costs, we have made firing into a hassle-free exercise.

Some people are convinced, in spite of the evidence to the contrary, that all those people who are fired in a downsizing deserved it. I remember discussing

---

[2] "Musings on Management," by Henry Mintzberg, *Harvard Business Review,* July/August 1996.

this question during a golf game with the president of an international bank. He was adamant that organizations do not fire good people, only the expendable low-performers. Maybe this makes the "survivors" feel better, but this sort of thinking only adds to the stigma of unworthiness borne by those people who have lost good jobs through no fault of their own. It is a system-wide disaster that damages individuals, organizations and society as a whole.

Recently, however, we have begun to see expressions of concern over the long-term effects of downsizing as a restructuring strategy. One of the reasons for this shift in attitude and in the willingness to terminate professional, managerial and executive staff, is the high cost of doing so. Even though there is a generally accepted upper limit of reasonable notice to which a departing employee is entitled, each settlement depends on many, highly individualistic factors. These can include any contract terms which may have been agreed to by the employee, length of service and position in the hierarchy. The scope of the settlement may include not only salary, but bonuses, benefits, pension contributions, automobile benefits, vacation pay and stock option plans. In a large-scale downsizing, severance costs must reflect the individual rights of all employees affected. Costs can rapidly mount up. In fact, it is not uncommon to see severance costs treated as an extraordinary item in a company's annual report, often explained in a special note. When downsizing is contemplated because of immediate financial pressures, management may back away because of the high cost involved. I know of several instances in which CEOs have chosen not to downsize or even terminate individual executives, because of the high cost of doing so.

SINKING TO THE OCCASION

The use of downsizing as a cost saving measure is becoming increasingly suspect because of its indeterminate long-term costs and its negative impact on those who stay. Before it became so popular, we used to refer to firing people as the industrial equivalent to capital punishment. The ultimate sanction available to a commercial organization, it strikes terror into the hearts of employees and their dependents. Its ripple effect traumatizes not only the downsized employee but all others as well. When people feel threatened, especially when that threat is caused by a human, rather than a natural disaster, it often brings out the worst in them.

Employment insecurity affects people in different ways, all of which are negative. Some people become subservient and passive. They do everything they can to be unnoticed. Some become political and try to gain favor with the people who "count," often at the expense of others. Some respond with anger, seeking overt and covert ways to take their revenge. Most people will become more cautious about the ideas they express, which works against the objectives of any organization that wants its people to be more innovative and risk taking. "Survivor sickness" is a well known phenomenon affecting organizations that have experienced a staff reduction. If the downsizing affected friends and long-time colleagues, it takes time for those remaining to deal with their sorrow, which will manifest itself in any number of ways, at an incalculable cost to the organization. And, of course, those who survive have to pick up the slack, taking on the added burden of the work of those who were downsized.

ALTERNATIVE WAYS OF CUTTING COSTS

More and more organizations are now finding that they need to replace some of the people who left in the downsizing. While this may reflect a return to a growing economy, it may also be an embarrassing admission that the staff cutting exercise was at least partly ill-conceived. You have to hope that this doesn't reflect a conscious strategy of replacing highly paid senior staff with lower paid junior staff.

Sometimes, however, short-term expense reduction is an inescapable economic requirement. When you can't meet the payroll and are unlikely to be able to do so in the near future, staff terminations may be the only possible action. But increasingly, organizations are finding alternatives to putting people out of work. The fact that we are becoming more reluctant to entertain mass downsizings as an improvement strategy is an encouraging sign of a return to a healthy perspective. Through a variety of alternative strategies (such as focusing on revenue growth, reallocating staff to the development of new markets and new systems, and sometimes just keeping people employed on maintenance and clean-up work), some organizations are managing to avoid wholesale layoffs. Strategies, including across-the-board salary decreases, can be used to keep the workforce together while the company reorganizes and reallocates staff. Anthony von Mandel, President of the Marc Anthony Group, may be in the forefront of a new trend when he says "I have long been a skeptic and critic of downsizing. From what I've seen, it's a strategy that takes out the heart, and puts a cap on the future, of many corporations."[3]

Retirement incentive programs have been widely used as an alternative to involuntary downsizing. These can be expensive because they usually include

---

[3] "You're (still) Hired," *The Globe & Mail Report on Business Magazine*, December 1996.

a lump-sum payment as well as on-going benefits coverage and pension rights. Another disadvantage is that highly valued employees may opt to leave when the organization would prefer they remain. The oldest and longest service employees tend to be the ones who leave, taking much of the organizational history and knowledge with them. Of all the costs, this may be the most serious, and it is the one that is least tangible and most hidden.

Nevertheless, voluntary incentives have been effective in reducing the staff complements of organizations that cannot sustain employment at previous levels, and they are certainly more humane in that they do offer a valid option to people who may want to go, but haven't made the break for financial or other reasons. Some people who have voluntarily retired under a such scheme have successfully launched alternative careers. Many have very positive feelings about their previous employer. My friend, Lino Magagna, was a career manager at a large electric utility who voluntarily retired under the company's scheme. He then launched a career as a contract consultant and project manager and has since enjoyed enormous success. While he is working every bit as hard as he used to, he feels he has greater control over the working part of his life. He also feels that his own skills have developed as a result of his need to market his services and sustain high levels of client satisfaction. Lino is one of the fortunate people who successfully seized the opportunity to change.

DOWNSIZING: A STRATEGY OF LAST RESORT

Many corporations that have avoided downsizing report that they engaged in open dialogue with their employees about the crucial questions of revenue growth, productivity and profitability. Those employees aren't likely to see profitability as a dirty word, and they probably have developed a keen sense of personal responsibility for contributing to the organization's business performance. It takes visionary and courageous leadership to hang on to people in the face of declining financial performance, since most executives are expected to include downsizing in their short-term recovery plan. But it is becoming more acceptable to search for alternatives to downsizing and we can expect to see and hear a great deal more about the subject. In this case, the proclivity of organizations to follow fashion may serve a good purpose.

While an awareness of the downside of downsizing will lead to more balanced decision making, we should not expect that all organizations will be able to avoid the need to lay people off in the future. As long as it is recognized as a strategy of last resort, it's a step in the right direction.

STRATEGIES TO ACHIEVE A MORE BALANCED APPROACH TO DOWNSIZING

1. Work *with* employees to avoid downsizing.

Middle managers and employees in most organizations have the most amazing capacity to accept reality if (a) it is honestly presented and (b) they have an opportunity to help shape the organization's response. The subject of employment insecurity, although it may not be discussed openly, is a close-to-the-surface issue. It doesn't go away if you don't talk about it. If anything, the insecurity grows worse in the absence of honest, open and realistic discussion.

A change manager at a major financial institution attributes most of her department's success to an open discussion of re-employment and severance packages with staff. This is the first step in the department's change strategy. She finds that it actually relieves anxiety to address the worst-case scenario openly, right at the first meeting. Then people can begin to contribute constructively to the change process.

The best results seem to occur when employees are involved in the creation of alternatives to downsizing, such as the development of new business, new systems and new ways of working. Even if that is not the case in a specific organization, employees deserve a chance to save their jobs through innovation and self sacrifice. There is a growing list of success stories about how employees worked with management to deal with the problems face on, to their mutual benefit.

Executives must be careful not to use the prospect of downsizing as a threat. That simply terrorizes and freezes employees. One CEO I know would frequently tell his people that they needed to change their attitudes or "all of our jobs are at stake." Employees initially found the message intimidating, and then, as in the story of the little boy who cried wolf, exaggerated and untrue. The problem was that the President didn't follow up his concern with any ideas as to how employees could, in fact, change their attitudes and respond constructively to the organization's declining fortunes.

Not all employees nor the unions that represent them are receptive to engaging in open-minded problem solving about the organization's circumstances. But if leaders are prepared to work with their people in an open and constructive way, people are capable of the most astounding creativity and effort, especially when it means avoiding downsizing.

2. Create innovative working arrangements.

Organizations that cannot sustain the same number of full-time employees have alternatives to dismissal. Retirement incentives may or may not be practical but if possible, they should be considered, even in publicly funded organizations. They generally provide an adequate return on the up front investment in relatively few years. Boards, however, have a tendency to perceive retirement incentive programs as just another employee giveaway. I have worked with several such boards, including a newly constituted board of two hospitals which were merging. It took considerable time and analysis for them to fully accept that a retirement incentive program was needed as part of consolidation. They wondered if they had the right to spend public money to underwrite the cost of the program, and worried that they would not be able to replace the resulting expertise. Ultimately, they supported the staff's recommendation. The program was offered, the adverse staffing effects of the merger were mitigated and the number of involuntary terminations reduced.

If it is necessary to downsize, it may be possible to outsource non-core services through the organization's own employees. This is not a new idea, but I am surprised by how infrequently it has been used as a way of softening the negative impacts of downsizing. To use a simple example, an organization might help its maintenance employees form a small company and provide it with a contract for services. The contract could be established so that the commitment of the original organization would decline over time, in expectation that the maintenance company would find other customers and improve its productivity. An approach like this meets the needs of everyone involved, while encouraging people to be more entrepreneurial.

The city manager of a fast growing community told me that the city had decided to launch an open tendering process for several municipal services, such as garbage collecting, and that the city's own trade unions were being encouraged to bid on the work as independent contractors. Despite the practical and legal impediments to ideas such as these, they deserve active consideration in situations where the alternative is dismissal.

3. If you must downsize, make sure that people are provided with adequate support.

It is unrealistic to think that downsizing actions will entirely disappear. We will continue to experience bankruptcies in the private sector. In the public sector, all levels of government are experiencing significant budgetary constraints which are likely to lead to more downsizing.

When dismissing groups of employees is unavoidable, then care must be taken not to underestimate their plight. Some will never work again. The fortunate ones will go on to greater things, others will have to settle for less interesting, less remunerative employment, and still others will be reduced to scratching out a living as temporary staff or short-term contractors. People are finding it tougher than ever to plan and execute a successful employment replacement plan. Employers are becoming ever more skilled at deflecting the hoards of employment applications directed at them. People need help both personally and professionally and organizations have a duty to ensure that it is provided.

Unfortunately, organizations that are terminating groups of staff also have a tendency to cut costs by restricting the level of re-employment counseling service they will fund. This is a double whammy for the unfortunate people who have been dismissed. Re-employment counseling is still a relatively new field. It has been around for little more than twenty years. People still misunderstand the role and value of these services. Re-employment counselors not only provide emotional support for people during the trauma which often follows dismissal, they apply professional skills to helping their candidates develop practical plans to search for alternative employment. Often, finding another job like the one lost is not a viable option. Good counselors will help their candidates explore options and alternatives. They also access sound business advice for those who are going to start their own businesses. Most of the better re-employment firms provide a range of services, including financial and retirement advice, psychological and vocational testing and all the core services related to conducting a job search. The services of a competent re-employment professional can be a catalyst to positive career change for displaced employees. Employers should question their own assumptions about the kind and amount of support required and be open to the advice of the professionals in the field.

CHAPTER 5

FAIRNESS—EVERYONE'S CORE VALUE

One of the distinctive things about being human is an unshakable belief in the concept of *fairness*. This value is ingrained, often unstated, and always involved in the events which command people's attention inside organizations. The value statements of many organizations are often written in the future tense. We must remember that they define the values that the organizations *intend* to adapt, not necessarily those which exist. So much is said and done about the subject of values that it is easy to forget that the values of any person or organization are what they *are*, not what they are *said* to be. But regardless of whether fairness, and its close cousin, equity, show up on the official list of values—they are at the heart of what people think is most important. They shape the perspective we bring to our working lives and the judgments we make about what is right and wrong.

In organizational life, our preoccupation with fairness both helps and hurts us. It helps us because it is at the heart of the civility we bring to our relationships and the emphasis that we place on balancing commercial and human considerations. In most organizations people expect (and normally encounter) decency, equity and principled behavior. On the other hand, the strength of our commitment to fairness can lead to problems. For many people, fairness means treating each individual absolutely equally. Even if that were possible, some people would find it objectionable because of the potential loss of individuality. People demand to be treated individualistically. So we immediately run into a logical dilemma. But an even greater problem arises from the fact that, while the value of fairness is virtually universal, interpretations of what constitutes fairness are highly divergent. Even people who work together and share many goals and experiences may have wildly different interpretations of the same events and situations. Managers who undertake an action or make a decision in complete good faith are stunned when accused of unfairness or inequity. So, while we know that virtually everyone values fairness, determining what is fair in real-life, day-to-day operations can be an elusive goal and an exercise in frustration.

DO NICE GUYS FINISH LAST?

In an increasingly global economy, this penchant for doing what is fair can be particularly confusing for people from other countries. For Canadian employees, fairness can be more important than efficiency, something which is intensely confusing and annoying for Americans who take commitment to profitability for granted. Americans do value fairness, but other principles may take priority. A U.S. business associate of mine became so annoyed at being challenged by our Canadian employees regarding business plans they deemed to be unreasonably optimistic, that she could not contain her disdain. Ken Polley, Chairman and CEO of Lindsey Morden, is one of the comparatively few Canadian executives who has led both Canadian and American organizations. He is deeply aware of the profound value differences in the Canadian and U.S. entities of the same company and, as a committed Canadian, he is worried about whether the Canadian economy can prosper if it elevates fair dealings at too great a premium over commercial success. Recently, Lindsey Morden integrated its Canadian and U.S. operations in one combined North American entity and Polley is constantly struck by the dynamics created by the clash of American and Canadian values. He sees the clash as highly energizing and expects it to be a useful catalyst in his company's North American integration and in ongoing development. He believes, however, that the Canadian participants in the group need to balance their strong commitments to fairness with entrepreneurial, more competitive values. The quickening pace of global competition, he cautions, places all economies at risk of being left behind, with the result that responsiveness, agility and competitiveness will be survival issues that need to be very high on a company's list of values.

Several years ago I was engaged in a joint venture with some international partners. As part of the arrangement I was a member of the Board of Directors of this company. Although we all got along well and did business together happily for some years, my colleagues found my ways quaint and occasionally baffling. My insistence on asking about the fairness of proposed actions certainly raised eyebrows and appeared to go against the grain. It wasn't so much that my business partners did not value fairness; it was more a question of emphasis and degree. To them the business of business was business. Other considerations were addressed only if they would not detract from the primary objectives of competing successfully and making money. I was very much aware that the emphasis I placed on the value of fairness was sometimes seen as a disadvantage in the hurly burly of competitive business.

IT'S SO EASY TO SEEM UNFAIR

Certain recurring situations bring this core value strongly into play.

SPECIAL ADVANTAGES FOR SENIOR MANAGEMENT

As countries and organizations move to become increasingly egalitarian, the manifestations of social distance within hierarchies can prove highly problematic. The perception that senior people in the organization are treating themselves more favorably than others is deadly. As discussed in Chapter 13, when executives argue that it is necessary to freeze or even roll back compensation, they need to be prepared to apply those actions to themselves. Or if executive perks are highly visible, arguments that the company needs to economize are likely to encounter a derisive reaction. When IBM removed the reserved parking spaces for executives from its company parking lot, employees applauded the gesture. Leaders with a common touch are far more popular than those who appear to see themselves as superior to the people they lead. Setting oneself above others strikes people as inequitable and therefore unfair.

COMPENSATION

Compensation, particularly pay for performance and variable income, is another area fraught with opportunities to stumble over everyone's core value. When employees, including management level employees, believe that someone else received a higher increase or bonus than they did, they are more inclined to attribute that to favoritism than merit. This very core tendency is nevertheless disturbing for those who believe in the motivational power of incentive compensation.

ELIMINATING ANYTHING!

Organizations will most definitely arouse complaints of unfairness if they decide to take something away. Decisions to reduce benefit coverage, increase contribution rates on benefits, change assigned work schedules, or even discontinue the practice of giving Christmas turkeys will cause distress. I don't know why people think it's unfair to take away what has previously been given, but employee reaction is quite unforgiving. One organization announced a new integrated compensation system embracing salary, incentives, benefits and perks. There were about a half a dozen significant improvements in various aspects of the program and only two ways in which the program had been carved back. The bulk of employee responses related to the two features which had been reduced in value; little was said about the improvements. Experienced executives and managers will not find this story surprising.

DISCIPLINARY ACTION

Chapter 10 examines the growing resistance to performance evaluation and criticism. When the issue becomes serious enough that discipline, such as suspension or even termination is involved, the stakes rise and divergent perceptions of right and wrong come into strong conflict. The sanctions of the organizations must be applied in a way that is perceived to be fair and consistent. There is a real question as to whether that can ever be accomplished.

TERMINATIONS

Employees hate to see people lose jobs, especially if they know the person terminated. They will be very critical if they suspect even a hint of unfairness in the way terminations are carried out. An employee population in one company was outraged when a 63-year-old sales manager was terminated a few weeks after a party held to celebrate his 25-year service anniversary and a few weeks before the Christmas season. The timing was perceived to be such a huge violation of standards of fairness that one wonders how the management team could have been insensitive enough to allow it to occur.

In another organization, a functional vice president fired his secretary for chronic bad performance. The rest of the organization's one hundred employees were stunned by the termination because they perceived that it had occurred completely out of the blue. I have encountered many similar situations and confess to some confusion about the basis for the employee reaction. Performance discussions between boss and subordinate are by nature confidential. Consequently, other employees are rarely aware of the efforts made to rehabilitate the performance of a low-performing employee. But for some reason, people tend to assume the worst; that the actions were arbitrary and heartless.

EMPLOYMENT EQUITY

The question of who gets which jobs and/or promotions is one in which people expect fairness to be a primary consideration. This is quite understandable, since jobs are like gold in the post-industrial economy. When there are fewer good jobs than qualified candidates, competition is intense and the employer's decision may displease many people. Concepts of fairness in employment are subtle. The past few years have seen a shift away from the principle of simply selecting the best candidate. Now other factors are addressed as well, such as the need to create a ethno-racially balanced workforce and the need to avoid sexual discrimination.

A strong trend, particularly in the not-for-profit sector, is to rely on selection committees to achieve greater fairness and equity. But there is no guarantee that their decisions will be perceived as superior to those made by individual managers. One thing is sure, any decision will be watched carefully and people will readily express any displeasure they may feel about the essential fairness of the process.

Legislatively mandated employment equity has been a controversial strategy of organization change, probably because it creates troubling value conflicts. Racial and gender bias is clearly unfair and wrong. On the other hand, the concept of reverse discrimination continues to raise concerns, regardless of how real a threat it may or may not be. People may find themselves in conflict between their commitment to equity and fairness to minorities and a belief that everyone is entitled to fair and equitable treatment, even if they are a member of the so-called mainstream. We want the best of both worlds—increased opportunity for under-represented groups, but not at the expense of those who are over-represented. When this is complicated further by mandatory program requirements such as employment equity and pay equity, the stakes increase and tempers may flare, giving rise to yet another conflict. One can be completely in support of the underlying purpose of employment equity, of removing discrimination from the workplace, and at the same time oppose employment equity legislation because it may be perceived as reducing important human issues to bureaucratically artificial solutions. Even so, employment equity has brought important questions of discrimination to the forefront. Because most people believe that discrimination is unfair, they have been willing to engage in open discussion of these contentious questions. In the process, they have learned just how discriminatory some of their practices and unspoken assumptions really are.

Some proponents of ethno-racial diversity argue that diversity is good business. This is a disturbing argument. It suggests that the reason to remove unfair discrimination from the workplace is to gain points for doing so (and hence, more business) from the increasingly diverse marketplace. While organizations known to be undertaking anti-racist initiatives may indeed achieve greater support from the affected groups, what happens if there is no direct business pay-back from diversity initiatives? Would that remove the incentive for doing so? Removing discrimination from the organization is the right thing to do for its *own* sake. Any increased sales and profits that might result is nothing more than a nice bonus, if it occurs at all.

ABUSE OF MANAGEMENT AUTHORITY

Bosses have enormous power. They can withhold rewards and, in extreme cases, make life a misery for those who report to them. While people may have to put up with that, they rarely do so willingly. Much of our literature replays the theme of good people as organizational victims. In literature, plays and films we see the executive portrayed as the epitome of all that is self serving. Len Deighton's highly successful trilogies, *Game, Set, Match* and *Faith, Hope and Charity* revolve around the efforts of his hero, Bernard Samson, to cope with vicious office rivalries and the political machinations of his superiors.

Our growing awareness of employee abuse may be the result of public attention to the phenomenon of child and family abuse as social issues. The notion that the people with the power must not be allowed to abuse it is certainly having an impact on the workplace, although to what degree is not yet clear. But nobody likes a bully, and it's likely that intimidation, harassment and disrespect will become less and less acceptable in workplace relationships mainly because they are unfair. Expressions of protest over the shrinking prerogatives and powers of managers can be expected, but probably will not amount to much.

The abuse of management authority is a subject we can expect to hear a great deal more about. Concerns over employee abuse will gain momentum and will change the definition of what is acceptable in working relationships. My friend, Peggy Cleary, recalls a meeting with her boss which took place after everyone else had gone home. At that meeting, she disagreed strongly with his point of view on the issue being discussed. He became more and more frustrated by her persistence and ultimately lost his temper. The angrier he became, the more intimidated she felt, to the point where she became frightened for her physical safety.

As the universal core value, fairness represents the standard that is most frequently applied to one's experience within organizations. Whether there is more or less fairness in today's organizational environment is an open question. So is the question of whether our endless search for fairness is good or limiting. Explaining to someone that life is not fair is rarely helpful. In any case, it makes no real difference since executives must lead within a context that insists that things be fair. The perception that something is unfair eats away at the very fabric of employee/employer relations until it pops up in some form that makes response unavoidable. It is far better to acknowledge the concern when it is first presented, even if executives can't do very much other than acknowledge the apparent lack of fairness and explain why rules of fairness cannot be applied in that particular situation.

STRATEGIES TO WORK WITH EVERYONE'S CORE VALUE

1. Make expectations and consequences crystal clear.

In his excellent book, *Healing the Wounds*, David Noer points out that the old employment "contracts" were based on expectations and a sense of entitlement that can no longer be fulfilled. The new employment "contract" is one in which the organization does not undertake to provide the level of security people have come to expect. Noer argues for explicitness in defining the new contract, to ensure that employees understand what the organization is and is not prepared to provide. If an organization makes it very clear that it should not be expected to provide career-long employment security, for example, then it is less likely to be thought of as unfair when it is unable to do so.[1]

The organization should also make clear how it deals with under-performing staff. This is admittedly a sensitive subject, and one that should be neither avoided nor over-emphasized. This aspect of the relationship between the employer and employee should be discussed in a forthright manner so that people understand that it involves mutual obligations. Explaining openly how decisions to terminate people are made and how checks and balances are applied is one way of dealing with this delicate issue. It helps to point out all of the ways in which the organization will help people meet required standards, but it must also be stressed that responsibility to achieve results belongs to individuals.

2. Test reactions to decisions and actions before finalizing them.

It isn't always possible to consult with people before decisions are made. Even when consultation is possible, it is not always possible to follow the advice obtained. Nevertheless, testing ideas before action is a good habit to get into, provided that the advisors are objective enough to provide reliable insight into the effects of the decisions.

Executives typically do consult prior to action, so it seems strange that they should be surprised at the negative reactions that invariably arise regarding those decisions that have been made without prior consultation.

---

[1] *Healing the Wounds*, David M. Noer, Jossey-Bass Inc., San Francisco, 1993.

This indicates the complexity of how Everyone's Core Value plays out in real life. It is prudent to try to develop as much advance insight as possible. And never assume people will see your intentions as pure and positive.

3. Invest in economic education.

Employees need to develop a more balanced appreciation of the importance of good financial and economic performance. If the importance of profitability is not clear to everyone, that should be addressed. It will be a long time before anything replaces fairness as a core value, but we do need to build the importance of other values, such as competitiveness and financial viability. This can be accomplished by helping employees develop a broader and deeper view of the issue of fairness in relation to the need for organizational sustainability. They need to appreciate that both are important. Senior managers may need to participate in the dialogue, to help create a broader understanding of the realities of organizational life.

4. Demonstrate respect for fairness.

There's nothing to be gained by throwing out the baby with the bath water. In spite of the difficulties it presents with regard to organizational effectiveness, fairness is a valuable consideration. It is part of what makes us distinctive. The fact that the value may manifest itself in enormously irritating ways does not justify leaders to be disrespectful of its importance. If someone perceives something as unfair, that perception will ultimately need to be addressed.

Leaders who demonstrate disrespect for fairness will lose the support of others. It's rarely necessary to accuse leaders of the majority of well run organizations of being unfair, because most bend over backwards to be fair. It's just that some people's definitions of fairness can be so surprising that leaders require iron self-control to avoid reacting with disrespect. It is permissible, even necessary, to debate whether something is fair or not, but it is not permissible to show indifference to the concern.

5. Address the issue of fairness through organizational communication.

The boards of two acute care hospitals in the same community had reached an agreement to merge their organizations and operations. Part of the implementation plan consisted of a staff selection process in which the most qualified person from either hospital was to be chosen. In announcing the process to staff, the two CEOs acknowledged that some people would wonder whether the process was fair. They explained their rationale that this was the fairest possible method. In doing so, they acknowledged the importance of the concern and the steps that they had taken to address it. Not everyone agreed that the selection process was completely fair, but the challenges were minor compared to what they might have been.

It's almost always better to acknowledge rather than ignore an issue that is raising concerns. If you must announce actions you feel may be perceived as unfair, consider addressing the issue up front. There is much to be gained by doing so.

PART II

THE ROLE OF LEADERSHIP

CHAPTER 6

LEADERSHIP—CHARACTER MEETS CONTEXT

Why do we love to loathe our leaders? One of the hottest topics in business journalism these days is leadership failure. This almost gleeful pummeling of unsuccessful leaders reflects and feeds a profound skepticism about the motives and competency of leaders in all sectors—business, government and not-for-profit.

- In 1996, the tribulations and ultimate resignation of the Chief of Staff of the Canadian Armed Services, General Jean Boyle, was headline news for days.

- The public release of Chief Executive Officer compensation in the Ontario public sector caused an outcry of indignation, as if there were something shameful and furtive about a level of remuneration that most business people would find totally unremarkable.

- Although people found the widely-reported squabble between the McCain brothers and their various offspring unseemly, few would deny that it was also titillating.

- President Clinton's much publicized Monica Lewinsky affair demonstrated that, while Trudeau's dictum that the government has no business in the bedrooms of the nation may be true, the reverse is most certainly not the case.

Leaders know that they will be the object of relentless scrutiny. We seize any sign of weakness or error on their part to confirm our expectation that they will ultimately disappoint us. And, when disappointed, there is no limit to our anger and contempt. We reserve a particularly harsh and unforgiving lexicon for leaders whom we perceive to have failed or misbehaved. We have always held our leaders to heroic, near impossible standards. And we invariably look back at them through rose-colored glasses. In lamenting the absence of great leaders from the past, such as Churchill and Roosevelt, people often forget how fallible and distrusted they were at different stages of their careers.

My own experience of organizational leadership seems to have been a great deal more positive than that of others. Moreover, the mixed results of my own forays into the world of leadership have served to sharpen my appreciation for the successes of others. I once heard William Dimma, then chairman of a real estate corporation, give a speech about the life of the CEO. He encouraged the audience to aspire to senior level responsibility and painted a compelling picture of how the professional and personal lives of CEOs become so highly integrated that the distinction between them tends to disappear. Mr. Dimma may not remember the occasion, but his audience of senior corporate managers was transfixed by the fascinating image he portrayed of a life of challenge and growth.

My picture of organization leadership is still an optimistic one. Senior people in organizations are, for the most part, decent and talented. Certainly there are exceptions, but that does not change the general truth. Leaders (by which I mean chief executive officers, other members of the executive team and board, and people with senior management responsibility) will be attracted to those organizations which provide the best setting for them to develop and use their talents.

LEADERSHIP IN PERSPECTIVE

Why then does good organizational leadership seem to be in such short supply and bad leadership so unfortunately plentiful? Perhaps it's because we see leadership as an individual quality; something that individuals either do or do not possess. The reality is more complex. Leadership does not exist in a vacuum. All leaders function in their respective context with a unique set of imperatives and constraints. Former American President Gerald Ford is one of many leaders to point out how little real power American presidents actually possess to make or enforce their policies; something we may find very difficult to believe.

Some organizations have consciously set out to constrain the prerogatives of their leaders. One nation-wide professional association was concerned that a succession of national elected presidents had each initiated their own pet projects. Each of these projects involved significant financial expenditure and scarce staff time, in ways which were seen to reflect the president's enthusiasm and not necessarily the will of the membership. In response, the organization formed a special board-level finance committee with sweeping and quite independent power to approve the national budget and *any* expenditure. Over the next few years, the finance unit effectively re-established financial control, but in the process it had itself developed as a competing power center in the association. The result, in the eyes of some senior organization participants, was fragmented accountability and cumbersome decision making. Nevertheless, that organization believed that it needed internal safeguards from its own leaders. A similar pattern can be detected in the growing regulatory constraint on executive compensation practices (discussed in Chapter 13) and in all the current attention being paid to board level governance.

THE CHARACTER/CONTEXT DYNAMIC

The literature of leadership is filled with prescriptions and advice on what to do and how to do it. It includes some excellent studies by writers and researchers whose ideas seem sound and helpful. A few hours in the business school library leaves us with the impression that the ingredients of effective leadership are clearly defined and well understood. But the problem is that we have come to regard success or failure as the result of leadership competence exclusively, even though we know that the effects of context on the ultimate outcome can be decisive. This simplistic view inevitably leads to a lack of trust in our leaders.

Effective leadership is a function of the interplay between the competence of leaders and their understanding of the specific environment in which they are working. By "context," I am referring to the external and internal environments in which leaders work. This includes technology, competition, industry structure, organizational history and values, financial resources, stockholder aspirations and, of course, those ugly politics. The "context" is the given situation, the situation over which the leader is unlikely to have control. The organization's accountability framework—the way roles, responsibilities, authorities and accountability are defined—is an important part of the context. Some leaders have enormous internal power; others must build consensus among internal power groups, boards and owners before they can act. "Character," on the other hand, refers to principles, values, leadership style, skills, competencies and personal attributes; things which are within the control of the leader.

Those leaders for whom I have the greatest respect are always the first to admit that the context in which they work is every bit as important in determining success as their own skills, competencies, character and values. There is a refreshing humility to that notion. These leaders are prepared to admit that not everything is within their control. This awareness gives them more freedom, more flexibility and greater accountability. It also frees them from the pressure to be perfect—an impossible goal that only constrains them from a full range of choices. Effective leadership is an ongoing process, not a perfect outcome. It is a process that requires self-correction and refinement according to the demands of the context. It allows for expanding rather than contracting the range of choice and action.

Our failure to understand the character/context dynamic leads to constant disappointment. When problems persist, we see them as leadership deficiencies. Some problems are so complex, so deeply rooted in factors transcending the influence of any single person or organization, that no leader can single-handedly solve them. Leadership of contemporary organizations is something that is shared by many people, not just the boss, and this gives rise to some of the thorniest, but most important issues that leaders face. When examining them, we should bear in mind that the conditions in which leaders work are highly dynamic, usually unclear and brutally demanding. Indulging ourselves in the general climate of anti-leader vitriol is not constructive. Effective leadership is an outcome, not a right; and there is much we can do to help leaders lead.

HOW CRITICAL IS IT TO KNOW THE CONTEXT?

The character/context dynamic suggests that effective leadership depends on deep knowledge of the organization's business. Without it, it is difficult for leaders to achieve credibility with colleagues. In fact, when their knowledge is more superficial than that of the people with whom they work, it is difficult for them to have confidence in their *own* judgment.

On the other hand, leaders who have grown up in one organization may be so imbued in the history and context of that organization that they fail to appreciate the possibilities or threats implicit in change. Long-standing leaders of organizations must be careful not to become complacent or resistant to change.

But if deep knowledge of the business is a pre-condition to leadership, how can we explain the success of so many leaders who are appointed from outside the organization? The answer seems to be that talented leaders are capable of quickly learning the essence of the business and industry, and know how to select the most reliable advice and counsel. Still, they are relatively vulnerable during the early months of their tenure. They must quickly acquire the background to know which problems are the most significant and which opportunities the most promising. They must do everything they can to shorten the period in which they must rely on the judgment of others.

Many leaders have pointed out that it isn't enough simply to be aware of the content and the context—strong leadership requires the ability to integrate these two. Michael Rayner, president of a professional institute, believes that one of his most important contributions as a leader is his ability to make the connections between the diverse ideas being discussed and developed at any time, find the common themes, integrate plans and programs and allocate resources accordingly. Barry Adamson, head of a major professional services company, would agree. He maintains that an ability to understand the external environment and ensure that the organization is well integrated with it is a key function which consumes much of a leader's time, regardless of the nature of the organization. This role of chief integrator is one that leaders are uniquely positioned to fulfill. It consists of identifying the connections so that people can make more effective use of scarce time and resources.

HOW THE LEADERSHIP LITERATURE PERPETUATES THE MYTH

If leadership is a function of both character and context, it is clear that there are as many environments as there are leaders. It is presumptuous—if not impossible—to offer advice that fits all cases. This is why many books on leadership focus on individual attributes and aspects of character rather than context. Jay Conger, for example, presents an analysis of charismatic and non-charismatic leaders in terms of the attributes which distinguish the two types.[1] Others, including Peter Drucker,[2] are more inclined to see leaders in terms of how well they perform certain functions such as planning and using time. Some of the more popular writers on leadership, like Warren Bennis[3] and Steven Covey,[4] see leadership as more a matter of personal character, and both emphasize the importance of ethics and principled behavior. With such

---

[1] *The Charismatic Leader: Behind the Mystique of Exceptional Leadership,* by Jay Conger, Jossey-Bass, Incorporated.

[2] Peter Drucker's books include *Concept of the Corporation,* 1993; *The Effective Executive,* 1993; *Management Challenges for the 21st Century,* and many others.

[3] Warren Bennis is the author of more than a dozen books on leadership, including *Leaders: The Strategies for Taking Charge,* 1997, and *On Becoming a Leader,* 1998.

[4] Stephen Covey's *Principle-Centered Leadership* (1991) and *The Seven Habits of Highly Effective People* (1989) are two of this extraordinarily prolific author's most popular titles.

luminaries focusing on only the character component of leadership, it's a small wonder that we underestimate the influence of context.

Experienced leaders are well aware of the tremendous effect that the context has on the results they achieve. When invited to discuss leadership challenges, they invariably talk first about their organization's environment and secondly about their actions or intentions. The context is systemic and cannot be ignored. It is rooted in the specific environment and circumstances facing a leader at any time. So why does leadership instruction focus more on character than context? Certainly all of the attributes—the skills, character, competencies and values—of leaders contribute to their success. But there is more to it than that and we do our future leaders a grave disservice by pretending otherwise.

CONFUSION ABOUT LEADERSHIP AND ACCOUNTABILITY

How many times have we seen leaders of our powerful institutions fail to take responsibility for problems or crises? Sometime subordinates are allowed to take the blame without support from people at the top. Does that not violate the unspoken contract we have with our leaders? Most of us have grown up in an organizational setting in which responsibility, authority and accountability are parts of a unified whole which shapes the context in which leaders work. We want to be able to assume that leaders willingly embrace the principle of accountability and apply it, not only to others, but also to themselves. We understand that positions of leadership involve great responsibility, which deserves generous compensation and other rewards of high office. Similarly, our experience of organizational life teaches us that it is the senior people, those with responsibility, who have the authority over those who toil in organizations. We may not like that, but we accept it. But the *quid pro quo* is that when things go wrong, the person who has the responsibility and authority to make decisions is the one who is held accountable.

When a decision is wrong, we naturally look to the person or group who made it. The fact that Harry Truman kept a sign on his desk saying, "The buck stops here" is one of the reasons people admired him. In fact, we admire willingness to accept accountability so deeply that it has become one of the most basic expectations of leaders—and an absolutely central aspect of the leadership context.

So what are we to make of leaders who accept the rewards of responsibility without the corresponding accountability? What is our contract with them? Or is this really only about self-interest, an inclination for leaders to protect their position by failing to support that of someone less senior in the hierarchy? It is impossible for us to know or fairly evaluate what goes on within the walls of a relatively secret organization. Such is the growing public cynicism about the quality of leadership that we tend to believe the worst.

We want our leaders to accept accountability willingly, to acknowledge their responsibility for success or failure, and to be prepared to accept the consequences for their errors and weaknesses. This is a very demanding requirement, particularly in contemporary organization life where the impact that leaders have on decision making is often less than it appears.

Our insistence that leaders be accountable sometimes finds expression in ways that are excessive. The regulation that makes directors of corporations in the case of business failure personally responsible for meeting the payroll, including income tax, can be unfair to public directors and ultimately self-defeating from the perspective of effective governance. But fair or not, we expect leaders to willingly assume personal responsibility. Those whom we perceive as trying to avoid it do not command much respect.

What we want from leaders is that they *share power and keep the account-ability*. In the current culture of consultation, we expect leaders to engage others, particularly those affected in decision making. Arbitrary dictatorial decision making has been replaced by consultative, consensual decision making. Empowerment is good; centralization of power is bad. These are the prevailing values of our time and leaders have to work within them. But empowerment must take place within a framework of policy and sound practice. When the delegated power is misused or abused, we hold the leader accountable, suspecting that the error occurred through deficient policy, training, information, or support. So today's leaders are expected to share the power and keep the accountability, even when that means taking the blame for actions of others, including people of whom the leader may not have been personally aware. After all, the leader is ultimately responsible for building an accountable organization, one which takes responsibility for its actions and the outcomes of those actions. How can true leaders behave any differently?

KEY EXPECTATIONS OF LEADERS

A balanced view of organizational leadership must deal with the inter-play of character and context and how it affects the way leaders approach some of the problems they find most challenging. I have great respect for many of the leaders with whom I have worked as a management consultant. I asked them to identify their most challenging organization and leadership problems and to describe how they had dealt with the problems and what, in the light of experience, they might do differently the next time they encountered a similar situation. They identified three main challenges: (1) guiding the organization into a successful future; (2) incorporating values in leadership and (3) modeling behavior.

ENVISIONING THE FUTURE

Although few characteristics are universal among leaders, the vast majority share an overwhelming commitment to the success of their respective organization. All of the chief executive officers I have met have been trying to the best of their ability to help their organization become more successful. Some are interested in their personal success as well. But none are indifferent to whether their organization succeeds. Their commitment is reflected in their expressions of what constitutes their principal role. Most agree that it is their responsibility to guide the organization into a successful future, whether that means "getting the strategic positioning right" or "coming up with a vision" or even "bringing the world down to the few key objectives we can build on." They recognize that the responsibility to establish the direction of the organization is theirs alone, no matter how extensive the consultation may be. And they feel the full weight of that responsibility. Many echo the sentiments of Ken Polley, Chairman of the Lindsey Morden Group, who is acutely aware of "how many lives are at stake" and how much "people depend on a company's success."

And the fact that leadership is increasingly seen as a shared responsibility does nothing to diminish the perception that leaders are the key architects of the future.

In order to make the successful future a reality, leaders need to be able to envision it clearly. What's more, they need to be able to share that vision with their people. The absence of a communicable future vision can cost leaders dearly in credibility.

Leading from vision is a concept which goes to the heart of contemporary leadership. If the leaders can't express their vision of the future, how can others contribute to its successful fulfillment? The most effective vision statements not only include a picture of what future success of the organization will look like in economic or business terms, but it will also show how the organization can create social value. For it is social value that will provide motivation for employees who are searching for meaning in their work.

LEADERSHIP AND VALUES

Jean Pierre LaRoche, a senior human resource professional with whom I have worked for many years, appreciates the importance of incorporating values, as well as vision, in leadership. When meeting with a group of fairly senior managers who had been brought into the organization from outside, he placed heavy emphasis on the values of the organization and how they were operational on a day-to-day basis. But it was clear to him that his remarks were having little impact on the new managers. In an effort to understand why, he requested feedback. These managers thought that values were abstract concepts of secondary importance that didn't need to be talked about at any great length.

LaRoche relates this to similar experiences he's had with other organizations. He is convinced that managers and executives tend to place the highest premium on pragmatic operational questions without reflecting on how they relate to personal or organizational values. He finds that values relating to the importance of consulting with employees before acting are a particular problem area. While managers may choose to consult, they often do so because they are expected to, not because it reflects their own values about how to manage. LaRoche believes that this failure to understand the importance of leading from key values and ensuring that these values are taken seriously as guides for action is a significant weakness in management.

LaRoche was involved in a search for a new regional director for his company. This experience dramatically revealed the importance of leadership and relationship skills. The selection committee surveyed all members of the regional staff to find out what factors they perceived to be most important in the selection of the region's new leader. Of the ten factors that emerged, only one was related to business or technology, and that was very general: the requirement that the new director have "the ability to learn our business." The other nine factors consisted of attributes of leadership, such as the ability to set clear direction, to implement the region's vision, and to consult skillfully with stakeholders in decision making.

LaRoche's experiences have convinced him that the most frequently missing pieces are leadership and management competencies rather than business and technical expertise. But most people assume the opposite. In view of the results of the survey, one member of the selection team advised his children to tailor their education to develop leadership and relationship skills in preference to technical and professional skills.

SERVING AS ROLE MODELS

Actions speak louder than words. How leaders actually behave in practice is a far more reliable indicator of what really counts and what is valued than are their pronouncements on the subject. Since most organizations have explicit values statements, senior people are watched very carefully to see how consistent their own actions are in relation to the values they espouse. Small mistakes and careless language have an importance far beyond the intention of the leaders involved.

For example, leaders of businesses often engage in government bashing. I remember with not much pleasure the interminable complaints about every single aspect of government policy during the lunch breaks of a management committee of which I was a member. This is an example of the narrowness of the executive view of life. It's not that government policy should not be debated. But when it is based on little experience of the other sectors of the economic system, it expresses an ingrown assumption of superiority that is too often encountered in the private sector. As leaders, I did not feel that we were modeling for ourselves or our frequent guests anything very constructive.

In many organizations, staff demand nothing short of perfection from their leaders. The truth of this daunting reality is readily evident in the surprised reaction of a leader who is told that a seemingly innocuous action or remark has prompted a highly judgmental response. Of course, executives are not always told about the impressions they create. The result is that employees can interpret messages and make judgments which are far removed from anything the leader intended. The modeling role of leaders needs to be emphasized far more in performance feedback and leadership education.

These three challenges inherent in the leadership context—leading from vision and values, developing relationship skills and always practicing what you preach—make the role of leadership intensely complex and demanding; far more so than the many critics in the media and elsewhere seem to realize.

LEADERSHIP STYLES THAT GO BEYOND STYLE

When working with leaders whom I admire, I am invariably struck by some distinctive talent or quality. It goes beyond style. In spite of all that has been said about style, it may not seem to be a very good indicator of leadership effectiveness at all. The following three leaders, for example, achieve outstanding results with very different styles. Anne Golden, the talented president of a major fund raising institution, applies abundant intellect and charisma to her very challenging role in a manner that fully engages the enthusiastic support of the volunteers and staff who work with her. Ken

Polley's patient, low key approach has been equally successful in fashioning his company into a global power and industry leader in insurance claims adjusting and related services. Jeff Mooney emphasizes strong teamwork and has developed a highly interactive approach in his food services company. In style, these leaders could not be further apart, but all have helped their organizations thrive. Most leaders I have worked with know they are not good at everything and try to work from a few key strengths.

However, it is valuable to examine two leadership styles which have emerged strongly in recent years—*leading from behind*, and *hands-on leadership*. The truth is that these emerging styles are not really styles at all. They are more accurately seen as approaches that have emerged to meet new expectations of leaders, and therefore they are part of the leadership context. In their own ways, they serve to influence and mirror changes in organization values and ways of working.

LEADING FROM BEHIND

Examples of "leading from behind" can be found in any kind of organization but are often encountered in a professional setting. The leader's role is that of executive midwife, helping others determine the emerging sense of direction, helping deliver it into a healthy environment and helping it gain momentum. The executive may serve a useful role as facilitator, summarizing the results of the group's discussions and encouraging the development of action plans that will move it to the next stage of realization. The leader avoids getting too far in front of thinking and would not be caught dead saying, "I know what to do, follow me!"

Those who practice leading from behind are on very solid ground internally since they are always closely in touch with mainstream thinking and are likely to find broad support for their agenda which, after all, is the organization's agenda. The disadvantage is that it isn't always the most efficient way to lead. It requires a great deal of patience on the part of the leader, who may have to wait until the organization is ready to commit to an action that may have been badly needed for some time. Since all wisdom does not reside with any one person or group of people, leading from behind may result in a lowest common denominator flavor, while long-term success may require bold and divergent thinking.

Some organizations offer no choice but to lead from behind. For example, the values of some professional partnerships in law/accounting/consulting are often centered in the individual responsibility of practitioners to make decisions as to how their actions meet professional standards. Traditional leadership authority may not have much place in such a culture. In political organizations or in those which represent a nation-wide federation of divergent regional interests, leadership action outside the current consensus may not be acceptable.

Not all leaders find leading from behind a satisfactory approach. It can prove particularly frustrating to those who have a clear vision about their organization's direction, for they will be unable to do much about it until others catch up. It requires great patience, exceptional listening skills and the ability to control one's ego. More and more organizations are choosing as their future leaders people with precisely those skills.

HANDS-ON LEADERSHIP

Another emergent "style" that is really an adaptation to current staff expectations is "hands-on" leadership. In this case the leader works face-to-face with individuals and groups at all levels of the organization in a highly involved manner. Hands-on leadership suits the skills and personalities of some, but not all, leaders and it certainly will trouble those who have a formalized sense of hierarchy, since hands-on leaders have no compunction about talking business with anyone with whom they come in contact. It can be highly motivating and challenging, since more people have the opportunity of sharing views and ideas with the top person, but it can also be intimidating to go up against such a powerful person in a face-to-face debate. Such leaders often have superb skills at making other people feel comfortable and valued.

At its worst, hands-on leadership can be disruptive, with the leader flitting from group to group, department to department, leaving a swath of instructions, opinions and sometimes contradictory messages. There is a real risk that intermediate levels of management lose importance in the eyes of employees who can go to the top person, and often the intermediate person is left to pick up the pieces if the leader's decisions and pronouncements conflict with previous decisions or policies. In very large organizations, hands-on leadership may be less practical; but even there, division managers and functional heads engage with a wider range of people and teams than they would if they stayed closer to the formal lines of communication. The increased use of inter-functional teams has probably brought most people into greater contact with people from very different parts of the organization and this has undoubtedly been highly beneficial.

Generally, hands-on leadership is much appreciated by people who feel flattered by the attention shown to them and their ideas, and most people enjoy having the opportunity to interact with various senior people. The caveat is that hands-on leaders may quickly wear out their welcome if they are prone to delivering monologues or pointing out the flaws in all of the ideas presented to them. Hands-on leadership has many strengths, perhaps because we tend to develop confidence and respect for those we have the opportunity of working with more closely. However, senior people must be careful not to over-identify with the views most recently expressed to them.

My sense is that we are seeing more leading from behind than hands-on leadership. The former is a natural consequence of greater empowerment and delegation. Leaders must take into consideration that more people within the organization are experiencing a sense of responsibility, a trend that seems to be motivated by the same factors as hands-on leadership. Consequently, leaders would be wise to demonstrate their interest and respect for everyone's thinking and to ensure that the best ideas are adopted, regardless of where they originate.

Both these newer approaches reflect a conceptual shift towards leadership as something that involves every person in every role. It is no longer perceived as the exclusive preserve of senior management. Increasingly, we believe that everyone can and should suggest constructive change, take responsibility for results, contribute to work teams and step up to the plate when they have useful knowledge or strong convictions.

Both hands-on leadership and leading from behind are responses to the context of modern leadership. Getting and staying in touch with perceptions and misperceptions has high importance on the leadership agenda. The elaborate formal hierarchies of the past can no longer be trusted as a reliable source of information and advice. They are suspected of distorting the meaning of the message. The response has been to strengthen the leader's own understanding of what is really going on within the organization. Some leaders may not feel entirely comfortable with these more interactive, less predictable forms of leadership. But the advantages, in terms of maintaining a working knowledge of the internal context, are so important that they would be well advised to put them into practice anyway.

STRATEGIES FOR ENHANCING LEADERSHIP EFFECTIVENESS

1. Focus on integration.

Integration involves the ability to recognize linkages within an organization and between an organization and its larger environment, so that steps may be taken to ensure that energy and resources are applied in a coordinated fashion. It is related to the systems theory of organizations as an open system constantly adapting to external and internal change and in which every action sets up a chain of reaction and consequence. No one is positioned as well as are leaders to integrate the many complex issues which need to be addressed. Information is funneled to the top and leaders have more ease of access to intelligence from other organizations and networks. They tend to be in contact with a broader cross section of the issues and influences that are relevant to success. Unlike other managers, they are not required to focus exclusively on one piece of the whole. Organizations, like people, are susceptible to being carried away by a particular enthusiasm or crisis. It falls to the leader to place things within a more balanced perspective, so that everything fits in and makes sense.

Leaders have a responsibility to constantly reshape the organization's view of its place in the wider world. Decisions about whether to undertake major interventions, such as restructuring, can be made only after considering their effects on other important initiatives and practices.

The ability to simplify things is another valuable talent. Similarly, leaders who are alert to duplication of effort provide a particularly helpful perspective in a world where everyone is encouraged to take initiative, and a myriad of task teams and projects are underway at the same time. The leader must be prepared to step in to eliminate committees and projects which have outlived their usefulness. Focusing on integration may be the most accessible opportunity many leaders have to contribute.

2. Set a high standard as a model for others.

This requires the development of self-awareness, without self-importance. Stephen Covey places special emphasis on the integrity of leaders.[5] Most employees I speak with agree that the credibility of senior people depends on their ability to demonstrate highly principled behavior, particularly under pressure. But being a good role model goes beyond principles. People scrutinize the behavior of their leaders for a glimpse into their character. Do they like to be agreed with or do they seem comfortable with strong challenge? Do they exhort people to maintain balance in their working and personal lives, while they themselves stay in the office on nights and weekends? Do they treat themselves better than others by, for example, securing employment for their family members in the organization? The leader of a publicly funded organization did so and people certainly got the message. There was a flurry of internal competition to "get your kids in for next summer." One key area of modeling

---

[5] *Principle-Centered Leadership*, by Stephen Covey, 1991.

lies in how leaders treat people. Those who speak disrespectfully of others should not be surprised to discover they are distrusted even by close associates who will wonder how that leader speaks of them behind their backs. This point may seem obvious, but I have been amazed to encounter senior people who speak in stunningly negative terms about other people in the organization.

The responsibility of the leader for setting the tone by example is relentless; it never lets up and there is no escape. It goes with the territory. And as the saying goes, "If you can't stand the heat, you should get out of the kitchen"—or in this case, the board room.

3. Share the power and keep the accountability.

Accountability is more than a platitude. People need to know what it means and how it works. What, for example, is meant by shared accountability? Or, can you guarantee that people who make risky decisions which fail will not be punished? It is fashionable to talk about encouraging more risk taking and learning from mistakes but people find it difficult to believe their mistakes will not be punished. It is essential that organizations go beyond the platitudes to clarify exactly what is expected and how accountability will be assessed in real life.

There are some traditional tools used to define accountability. Position descriptions often have an accountability section setting out limits of decision making authority and the results for which the incumbent is accountable. Performance contracts can be used to specify the expected outcomes. Performance criteria can be helpful. The model of board governance established by John Carver depends on the board setting clear performance criteria from which the accountability of the CEO can be determined.[6] Though helpful, these tools are unlikely to deal very well with the underlying question of what happens when things go wrong.

When people are caught up in the enthusiasm of decision making, it is difficult to focus attention on how blame will be apportioned if things don't work out. After all, that constitutes negative thinking in a world in which anything negative is considered demoralizing. But leaders and their staffs should talk about what accountability means to them in relation to the real work they do together. Most importantly, people need to trust the leader's willingness to stand behind them when they use their delegated power.

---

[6] "Boards That Make a Difference," by John Carver, *Jossey-Bass Nonprofit Sector Series*, San Francisco, 1990.

And it works both ways. If subordinates are unwilling to accept account-ability for their actions, leaders need to intervene, since unwillingness to accept accountability is often a negative signal about the way people are approaching their responsibilities. Mistakes are usually the result of a combination of systemic and individual factors. The fundamental responsibility of those involved is to prevent recurrence of similar problems. This means looking beyond the human error and thinking more deeply about the causes—in training, communications, information flow and other key issues. Are people working under such pressure that mistakes are inevitable? Are we asking more of people than they are equipped to give?

Leaders cannot escape their accountability because they are ultimately responsible for creating the environment within which the work is done. Nor can the person who made the error. Since responsibility and accountability are shared in most working environments, accountability systems must provide for working openly with colleagues to make the necessary changes, so that future problems are prevented.

4. Simplify the leadership lifestyle.

Corporate leaders who appear to use company assets to support luxurious lifestyles are met with growing animosity. I am not referring to rich executive compensation packages that result from the creation of wealth and share-holder value. I am referring to lavish corporate lifestyles such as are reflected in office accommodations, company-owned apartments, private jets, access to company-owned sports and entertainment tickets, use of private chauffeured limousines and so on. These practices are increasingly questionable in a society where the gap between the haves and have-nots is widening and in organizations where downsizing may have cost many people their jobs. Writing in the *Harvard Business Review*, Henry Mintzberg deplores the "disconnection between the management and the managed."[7] In the same article, he wonders why salaries of executives increase as a consequence of actions they take to fire front-line workers and middle managers.

Some executives are generally restrained in their enjoyment of the perks of office. The president of a company I worked for many years ago was redesigning his own office. He wanted it to be exactly the same size as the offices of his vice presidents, and relented and accepted a slightly larger office only when the vice presidents pleaded with him to do so. This was one of several manifestations of his lack of pretension as a leader and had a great deal

---

[7] "Musings on Management," by Henry Mintzberg, *Harvard Business Review*, July/Aug 1996.

to do with the fierce loyalty and respect he commanded. His attitude would fit very well with today's conditions.

It is common to rationalize some executive perks as being necessary to help CEOs deal with their incredibly busy schedules. And there is probably some truth to the fact that the time and energy demands on leaders are enormous. But living one's working life like a Middle East potentate raises questions about the values, and possibly the integrity, of leaders. Each leader will have to make his or her own decision about what perks and luxuries they feel entitled to, but they should do so with a clear understanding that luxurious corporate lifestyles may contribute negatively to the social distance and real accessibility of organization leaders, to their ultimate detriment.

5. Respect the time pressures of others.

Several years ago, my partner Brian Morrison and I conceived the idea of researching something we called "organizational downers," the experiences that people find particularly discouraging and de-motivating. We figured that if we could isolate those that are most soul-destroying, we could develop positive techniques to avoid or mitigate them, to everyone's benefit. Before the project was shelved in the press of other priorities, we had talked to people in more than a dozen organizations about downers and discovered that high on the list was being asked to do work that was not really very important. One person remembered having been asked to do an urgent analysis of how well a new business process was working. She worked nights and weekends over a two-week period and submitted a report only to learn that the manager had lost interest in the subject. Even though the incident had occurred several years prior to our conversation, her memory remained vivid and her anger strong.

Many people expressed strong resentment at being asked in a very casual manner to do seemingly unimportant tasks that nevertheless required great effort. Respecting the effort required of most tasks is one way leaders can show respect for people.

6. Encourage leaders at all levels.

In some organizations, leadership is viewed as a shared function, applicable to almost everyone who works there. In one accute-care hospital, for example, everyone is expected to develop three hospital-wide competencies: customer service, clinical skills and leadership. The hospital invested heavily in a consultative process, the goal of which was to define each of the competencies in practical terms so they could be used not only as a guide to action, but as a basis for individual development. It is easy to see that every manager has a leadership role, but at this hospital, everyone was expected to contribute to leadership of the hospital according to their abilities and their opportunities. In team meetings for example, it was not only the facilitator who was responsible for supplying the leadership impetus, it was the person whose experience and insight positioned him or her to step up to the leadership role, even if it was only for purposes of the specific point under consideration.

Each leader should define what leadership means within the context of that organization, and having done that, should communicate the function of leadership widely. It is an inherent function of many jobs, not just those of the executives. Key leadership roles are relevant to many, if not most, jobs. To treat leadership as if it were some mysterious quality that some people have (and others do not have) is limiting. We need to be able to discuss leadership in simple, inclusive terms that are meaningful to everyone.

Everyone needs a sense of direction, preferably one that is highly integrated with the larger organizational strategy. Every leader needs to develop understanding and buy-in for his or her goals. Helping others clarify and reach goals, helping remove impediments and obtaining resources are all part of leadership. The complexity and scope of leadership certainly increases as people rise through the management ranks, but the responsibility to provide leadership is found at every level, in every unit, and within almost every job.

7. Learn how to be leadable.

There is no such word as "leadable," but there should be. We need to remember the truth of the maxim: *we get the leaders we deserve.* We can help establish an environment in which leadership can flourish and grow, or we can tie our leaders' hands so tightly that we doom them to failure.

Good leadership is cause for celebration. We have every right to take personal satisfaction in the success of our leaders. After all, we contribute to their success by being leadable. That the opposite is true should give us pause. While it is sometimes true that we contribute to good leadership by strong challenge, it is also true that a hostile and uncooperative environment reduces the prospects of effective leadership.

There are several key ways people in organizations can contribute to good leadership. We can help others understand the way that consultation works. Consultation should mean openly providing information and suggestions to help the leaders make the most informed and effective choices.

It also helps when we operate from the assumption that leaders do weigh the information and alternatives and make choices based on all of the considerations. We can moderate our own suspicion and cynicism. We might ask ourselves why leaders would want to do the wrong thing or make the wrong decision.

Our greatest contribution to good leadership can be in influencing the environment in which our leaders operate. Forcing leaders to perform in a fish bowl, like politicians do, is against our own interests. We want leaders to do the right thing, which is sometimes the tough thing. But then we have to be prepared to accept that our leaders sometimes have to make unpopular decisions. Otherwise, the risk is that their need to communicate a popular outcome might outweigh the importance of the right outcome. While we may say we are repelled by "leadership by public relations," we may unintentionally contribute to it. If we punish honesty in communications by leaders, do we have any right to complain about dishonest communications?

As Thomas Edison once said, "Genius is one percent inspiration and ninety-nine percent perspiration." In the case of leadership, the relationship between context and content is more balanced. Unfortunately, the context receives less attention. No doubt this is because it is complex, ambiguous and often frustrating. It is easier to fall back on the simplistic idea that leadership is a function of the person, that it is a talent given at birth that can be honed through training and experience. While that view is not incorrect, it is incomplete.

The real question is how gifted leaders *apply* their gifts to the context. That is what will lead to their ultimate success or failure. We are expanding our understanding of what constitutes leadership and, in the process, are coming to the realization that all of us share the responsibility to foster it.

CHAPTER 7

THE CULT OF CONSULTATION

People now expect to be consulted; they feel entitled to a voice in decision making. It is almost inconceivable that leaders would make any important decisions before they check with people who might be affected.

But it wasn't always this way. We are now so accustomed to building consultation with stakeholders into our plans and actions that we may forget how recently we adopted this type of approach. Certainly leaders such as Henry Ford and Frederick Taylor never considered incorporating consultation into an organization's culture.

The culture of consultation has several roots. About two decades ago, North American companies came to the realization that they were losing market share to international competitors, largely because of the issue of quality. Other countries seemed to be able to produce better products without higher costs. When North American companies analyzed why, they discovered that other industrial systems, like the Japanese, used significantly different processes in which employees were not only welcome to contribute their ideas, they were expected to do so. This was an inherent part of the understanding between employees and employers. This realization led to a great surge of interest in ways of encouraging employees to express their ideas and suggestions about the work they do.

A variety of approaches to consultation has sprung up over the past 20 years—quality circles, suggestion plans and workplace meetings. As companies came to realize that their front-line staff often knew more than virtually anyone else about their customers, they began to involve more of those people in decision making and customer service innovation. This is one of the sources of that dreaded word "empowerment" which companies have applied to customer service roles by providing front-line staff with authority to resolve problems on the spot. The increased power of front-line staff has often resulted from broad consultation processes in which people have been asked to identify what they require for greater effectiveness in customer service roles.

The organizational development field has also contributed to the tendency for more and broader consultation. The importance of OD has been growing over the past two decades, and employee consultation is at the heart of the OD value system. OD specialists tend to be strongly committed to the importance of humanistic values in organizational life. For years, they've been advocating more democratic workplaces in the belief that to involve junior staff in decisions that affect them is a superior way of managing even the largest organizations. OD has also contributed its values to the newer field of organization change, in which encouraging employee input figures very highly. In fact, employee involvement is one of the most fundamental beliefs of organization change specialists, ranking right up there with vision and other methods of defining organization purpose.

The field of politics has adopted the practice of consultation with a passion. Can you imagine any modern day politician doing anything without knowing where public attitudes lie? Or, doing anything without promising extensive consultation before key decisions are made? It is difficult to know whether politics borrowed the art of consultation from business, or vice versa, but it is clear that consultation has developed as an inescapable part of the way things are now done in virtually any organizational setting.

But we still have a lot to learn about how to make it work for everyone involved.

WHY THE AMBIVALENCE?

Jean Pierre LaRoche, a senior human resource executive, believes that the way in which a senior executive consults with others is one of the most important expressions of personal values. To request a subordinate's advice or opinion is an act of respect. Conversely, to fail to do so may be an act of disrespect. So for LaRoche, then, consultation is seen as far more than a technique; it is the exercise of a fundamental value. Having witnessed countless examples of how the failure to consult has led to a weakening in support and respect for leaders, he firmly believes that knowing when and how to consult is one of the most important leadership skills, and one which can be gained only through experience.

While I've worked with many executives who sincerely want to know what others think about key organizational issues, they tend to have a love-hate attitude towards management by consultation. For people trained in the school that places leaders on a pedestal to take charge and show others the way, consultation can look and feel wimpy. They may have tried to be more consultative and found the results disappointing. They probably grew impatient with protracted discussions of ideas, which seemed to them to be a waste of time. And it certainly doesn't help when people use consultation processes as an opportunity to blow off steam or as a general beefing session. The truth is that the quality of thought that results from broad consultation isn't always very good. When the ideas are unusable, leaders may rightly sense that they are in a worse position than if they had never consulted in the first place.

However, genuine and sincere consultation has an important place. The proof of this can be demonstrated by the criticism, resistance and lack of buy-in that inevitably result when a leader fails to consult on an issue in which people feel that they have a stake. And, if lack of consultation becomes a pattern, then it is a pretty sure bet that cynicism will grow and leadership credibility will decline. For people no longer regard being consulted as a courtesy or an opportunity, but as their *right*. The question is not whether to consult, but how to make the consultation effective. This is not a simple task. There are many reasons why even the best-intentioned consultation can be derailed.

WHAT CAUSES BAD CONSULTATION?

Most of the underlying problems that give rise to poor consultation can be avoided or addressed when they occur.

PHONY CONSULTATION

Consultation that is undertaken for political expediency without any intention of following through on the feedback received is worse than not consulting at all. People will distrust and resent a consultative process if they think that the decision has already been made before their views were solicited. This should come as little surprise. Phony consultation is disrespectful and deserves the contempt it receives.

In one not-for-profit organization, a request by the Board for input from the Standing Committee on Long Range Planning was suspected to be nothing more than a token exercise. This led to the resignation of several long-standing committee members, which significantly damaged the credibility of the Board. This fiasco could have been avoided if the Board had given genuine consideration to the committee's suggestions. Ironically, the planning initiative under consideration would have required little change if the committee's suggestions had been taken into account. This scenario is repeated time and again in organizations. It is so unnecessary.

MIXED MESSAGES

Perhaps the most fundamental problem associated with consultation arises from the different expectations on the parts of those who are asking for advice and those who are giving it. Leaders may be perfectly clear in their own minds that they are requesting advice alone, with the intention of weighing everyone's views carefully and then deciding on a course of action. On the other hand, people who have been consulted often expect their advice to be followed, simply because it had been solicited. In some cases, they may imagine that they are actually being asked to *make* the decision. A great many people don't understand the distinction between consultation as a process of obtaining advice prior to a decision by the leader, and consultation as a form of collective decision making. When working with clients, I usually try to clarify the respective expectations of leaders and those consulted. It is sobering to experience, as I often have, how frequently leaders and their advisors start off with a very different understanding of the consultative process itself.

NO SENSE OF PRIORITY

It sometimes seems that all issues are assigned equal importance, so that being involved in a team examining the strategic direction of the organization, for example, should command no more attention than one dealing with job evaluation, and that both command the same attention as a team considering the office layout. When there is no controlling influence to maintain an appropriate sense of balance and scale to the consultation, people quickly lose interest and respect.

TOO MUCH OF A GOOD THING

When consultation as a leadership tool is overused, people grow more reluctant to participate. Far from feeling flattered that their opinion is sought, they are frustrated by the number of issues which they are expected to consider.

Similarly, certain consultative approaches are overused. For example, there is a growing distrust of the trend towards "leadership by survey," which is an unflattering reference to the tendency of some political leaders to undertake only that which surveys indicate people will support.

While most people value being involved in important questions affecting the well-being and future of their organization, they are increasingly troubled by the high costs the consultative process places on them personally. Some organizations have such a profusion of consultative efforts going on at any given time that people are forced to choose which meetings they will attend and which they will have to miss. This only adds to their frustration.

CONSULTATION MAY NOT COME NATURALLY

The ambivalence of many leaders towards consultation stems partly from their conflict between the respect they have for the consultative process and their sense that, as leaders, they ought to be taking a decisive posture on key issues. Leaders, after all, are expected to lead, so it is understandable that they may equate a consultative approach with abdication of their responsibility to decide and act as they think best. Well aware that the right decision is not always the popular decision, they may wish to avoid limiting their freedom to act according to their own best judgment.

Another problem is that some CEOs must answer to Boards whose focus is very results oriented and whose patience for poor results is limited. This places great pressure on the context within which broad consultation might be considered. The truth is, effective consultation is time-consuming. It requires great patience and flexibility. The CEO may not feel that he or she has the luxury to consult about something that needs to be done *now*.

And when all is said and done, there will always be someone who is unhappy with the results. No matter how committed the leader may be to the process, no matter how sincerely he or she tries to listen, some people will insist that the process was flawed. Sometimes the benefits of consultation are not as readily evident as the costs and frustrations.

GIVING FEEDBACK

People who have been consulted in an organization process frequently express dismay about the lack of feedback as to how their input made a difference. In spite of the fact that the importance of feedback is well understood in most organizations, it just doesn't always happen. There is no excuse for such a lack of courtesy. If the ultimate decision differs from the advice received, leaders may be reluctant to explain, and possibly defend, why. However understandable this may be, it is bound to cause more resentment than simply stating the truth of the situation—that the input was valuable and appreciated, and that the leaders made the decision that they felt was best in consideration of *all* the factors.

POLITICIZING THE CONSULTATION PROCESS

Leaders may be subject to the same pressures as those they lead. If they suspect that they are being used by a special interest group to promulgate a particular agenda, they will lose faith in the consultation process. Indeed, consultation may be inappropriate when approached on the basis of a single issue, or when there is a vested or conflicting interest on the part of those being consulted.

For example, it is probably appropriate to consult people in the design of the compensation programs and arrangements, but not about the amount of compensation.

CONSULTATION AS POLITICAL CORRECTNESS

Some people and some groups believe so strongly in the sanctity of consultation that the subject takes on a kind of political correctness. This raises highly sensitive issues, especially if people are convinced that decisions reached by consultation are by definition better than those reached in other ways.

The fact is, the dynamics of a particular team or group can lead discussion in the wrong direction. We have all experienced situations in which a dominant person with a particular mission or agenda has "captured" a consultation process. A related problem is that people are sometimes asked to offer advice in areas they may not fully understand. For whatever the reasons, some advice and recommendations that come out of a consultative process are not very good at all.

What is to be done when leaders, having urged people to become involved, are saddled with a wealth of useless advice that misses the point? The tendency is for them to try to convince people that their ideas have been used when such is not the case. This horrible situation has caused many senior people to question the wisdom of consulting in the first place. It has also led to some mind-bending communications designed to persuade people that it is impossible for their "terrific" ideas to be implemented at present.

In their effort to be "politically correct," executives will sometimes allow themselves to be talked into sponsoring broad-based consultation with people whom they do not fully trust. For example, one executive director of a unionized organization was skeptical as to whether or not union objectives would dominate the recommendations of a series of task teams working on an organizational change process. My assessment was that the recommendations had been arrived at independently by employees and did not unduly reflect the union agenda. However, the executive director failed to overcome his skepticism, and offered only partial support for the resulting recommendations. This was a flaw that seriously damaged the effectiveness of the process.

More and more I am encountering situations where leaders succumb to the impulse of their colleagues to undertake broad consultation, but do not really support the process in their hearts. We need to go beyond the mindlessness inherent in the belief that consultation is always a good thing. Not only do we need to be more selective about when to consult, but we need to give careful thought to how that consultation is planned.

Consultation is not a simple process. It can fail for all kinds of reasons, not all of which are within the control of the senior management team. But successful consultation can lead to exceptional results. It can unleash energy like few other techniques. It can surface truly innovative ideas. And it can do what it is most often intended to do—build buy-in for important organization directions and decisions. As a management technique, it has few peers in its potential for mobilizing effort and commitment in a unified direction. It has the potential to attract the admiration and support of colleagues from every level of the organization. It is certainly worth the effort to learn to do well.

CONSULTATION METHODS

Every leader has an informal network of inside and outside people whose advice they respect. They will draw on the advice of these people as they choose. Some extend their network of advisors through a myriad of techniques—"hot seats," management forums and special task teams. In order for leaders to fulfill their important role as integrators of diverse perspectives, it makes good sense for them to include as advisors people or groups who are known to oppose certain ideas. The better they understand the basis for opposing views, the more likely they are to find integrative solutions.

A variety of methods of consultation have come into use. Some, of course, have been misused. The two most common methods are surveys and focus groups.

SURVEYS

Questionnaires and surveys can provide a useful source of information about opinions and attitudes. Unfortunately, there is a tendency to both overuse and misuse them. People have been asked to respond to too many surveys on too many subjects, with too few results. They've grown weary of the process. They find it frustrating, especially in cases where they perceive that the underlying issues are not sufficiently important to warrant the time involved, or where they expect their leaders to decide such issues on their own. Sometimes the questions address complex issues by assuming a certain level of previous knowledge which the respondent doesn't have, or the questions are excessively broad, or ambiguous, or leading, or generally not well worded.

It is time to cut back on the use of surveys and questionnaires in order to avoid respondent burn-out. Save them for truly significant issues.

FOCUS GROUPS

The term "focus group" developed originally in the field of market research and has since been corrupted to refer to any facilitated group discussion. Like survey questionaires, focus groups have their uses and abuses.

They can be very useful to generate a full exploration of the participants' views on a subject under discussion. They can also serve to deepen and broaden understanding of the issues associated with that subject. When Ted Baker, a business unit manager at Lindsey Morden, was asked to develop recommendations to improve inter-business unit communications, he chose to speak to front line employees in a series of informal discussion groups that took place in several of the company's offices from coast to coast. The focus groups were highly instrumental in helping him develop his recommendations, mostly because he was so strongly affected by the emotion behind the participants' pleas for improved communication. That experience enabled him to speak with conviction and confidence, which made him a powerful advocate for the ideas he was presenting. When decision makers participate as facilitators and note-takers in focus groups, they can gain a sense of the level of emotion behind the views expressed. Focus groups can also be useful to generate ideas and test reactions to proposed courses of action.

Because it is difficult and time consuming to summarize the results of group discussions, focus groups are not well suited to developing quantitative knowledge about the distribution of opinions on issues within the organization. The use of focus groups can also create expectations on the part of participants for action and follow-up which may not fit with the leaders' intentions. It is always challenging to decide who should participate in focus groups, especially considering how difficult it can be for the facilitator to prevent the discussion from being skewed to reflect the attitudes of the participants.

Recently, employees seem to be resisting invitations to become involved in focus group discussions. Mike Raynor, president of a national professional institute, maintains that leaders should strongly urge people to participate, even when they initially decline. One reason is that people tend to forget that they were offered the opportunity to participate, and later blast management for initiatives with which they don't agree.

STRATEGIES TO CONSULT EFFECTIVELY

Consultation is not only a cultural imperative in most organizations, it is an essential feature of contemporary business life. As an approach to leadership, it is far more difficult than it may appear. People come to work with the expectation that they will be consulted. Leaders ignore this at their peril. While it is certainly possible to be non-consultative and survive as a leader, such a leader requires considerable compensating qualities.

Of the following tips for successful consultation, the first is the most important. It is so important, in fact, that it deserves to be a cardinal rule.

1. **Clarify what use will be made of the results achieved, even in cases when it is not possible to follow the advice received.**

2. **Consult only when the input will affect the ultimate result.**

Consultation for its own sake is *not* a good idea. At one end of the spectrum, we find leaders who consult simply because they like to stay in touch with the thinking of others. Some may do so in order to determine whether an insight or idea merits serious consideration. Sometimes they wish to have feedback on how some action was perceived, or how well some previous decision or investment is holding up. At the other end of the spectrum are those leaders who are fully prepared to live with whatever consensus view emerges from the consultation. Somewhere in between are the leaders who may be open to advice on how to implement a particular action, but not on the action itself. Of course, leaders will find themselves at different places on the spectrum at different times, depending on the situation.

Consultation is a good idea only when the resulting opinions and suggestions will truly affect the outcome and when the issue is important. Many issues don't require much consultation. The pendulum appears to be swinging back to a more balanced understanding of when consultation should and should not take place.

"Affecting the final result" does not mean that the ideas will necessarily be implemented. As long as they are seriously considered, it is acceptable for the final decision to rest with the leader.

3. **Clarify expectations.**

People need to know what their role is. Are they being asked to participate as advisors or deciders, as part of a sample or as sources of suggestions and innovative ideas? Clarifying who is going to make the decision and how it is going to be made is almost always a good idea. Are they being asked to help make a decision or how best to implement a decision or how best to communicate a decision? Who will be making the final decision—the president, the marketing committee, the Board, the quality committee, the vice president of marketing, or the majority of employees? If these questions cannot be answered clearly, then the consultation plan needs more work.

4. **Provide participants with an open consultative process and feedback on how their contribution was used.**

This seems like an obvious point, one that should really go without saying. But it often happens that people devote their best thinking to an issue and never hear whether or not it was helpful and, if so, in what way it contributed. This is one of the seemingly small things about organizational life that is profoundly disappointing. Some feedback should always be provided, whether it is in the form of a copy of a proposal, notes from a focus group, or a simple telephone call. In the event that the input received was not helpful, providing feedback can be very tricky. Simply thanking contributors for their ideas is usually adequate. If people insist upon knowing why their suggestions were not adopted, they deserve a straightforward, but respectful reply.

5. **Select an appropriate consultation method.**

In many organizations, this suggestion would result in a moratorium on surveys and discussion groups. It would also encourage the increased use of the normal work teams as a source of advice and counsel. E-mail can also be used as a powerful consultation tool. If we provide people with relief from grinding away at too many issues in too many meetings of questionable importance, we may be able to recapture their keen participation in those processes where they can really make a contribution.

6. **Engage leaders in face-to-face consultation.**

The role of the modern president has been described as consisting exclusively of communications. That is certainly an exaggeration, but face-to-face contact is an important means of developing and sustaining a substantive understanding of the prevailing range of views. Participating personally in the consultation process is a good idea. It often provides an emotional dimension that is not afforded by other forms of consultation (which may be why some leaders shy away from it). This approach can be superior to the kind of arm's-length version of the truth presented by formalized market research.

It is not always possible for leaders to participate in face-to-face consultation due to time and geographical constraints as well as other factors. But, when possible, it helps them avoid the peculiar phenomenon that seems to arise whenever managers and executives attend sessions to hear the results of market research studies. If you have ever attended such a session, then you are no doubt familiar with the enormous amount of time spent trying to understand the meaning of the statistics and analysis provided. Such sessions tend to deteriorate into a kind of game as self-appointed statisticians try to find holes in the researchers' work. As much fun as this might be, it diverts attention from the results and insights the data provides.

When senior people have been a part of the process of generating the insight, their level of commitment to solving problems is much higher. It may be intimidating to have the company president participate in your focus group, but it can also be exciting and dynamic. Whether people remain inhibited is partly a function of the leader's skills, which can be developed. When leaders are privy to the opinions, perceptions, assumptions and feelings of people within the organization, they can deal with almost all internal and many external issues with complete confidence and decisiveness. They will be seen as real people and, therefore, as good leaders.

7. Seek ways to make consultation fun.

In 1995, a national professional institute decided to develop a new statement of organizational values. A task team was asked to facilitate a consultative process to achieve this. After the individual team members had spoken to most of their colleagues, a draft statement of values was developed. Then the fun began. Each and every employee was invited to attend the same one-day session in order to develop consensus. What made the day so engaging was the use of up-to-date computer technology to help create instant consensus in a real-time environment. The 150 participants were divided into 10 groups. Each person had his or her own keypad so that straw votes could be conducted and the range of opinions presented instantly. This allowed the areas of consensus to be easily identified, so that the workshop could focus on the areas requiring more thought and discussion. Each group was assigned one of the values and the responsibility of suggesting a revision to the draft values statement which was submitted to the entire workshop for a vote, with the results conveyed instantaneously. The result was both enjoyable and effective. By the end of the day, not only had a revised set of values been developed which most people could support, but a plan of action had also been defined. The organization had made an enormous investment in the process, by involving all the employees in one room on the same day and by employing technology to facilitate their work. But it was worth it. After the workshop, the task team was easily able to finalize the value statement and to provide all employees with feedback on the end result, in the form of a values statement.

CHAPTER 8

UP FRONT, IN CONTROL AND ARTICULATE: THREE IMPERATIVES OF SUCCESSFUL LEADERSHIP

Being a highly skilled leader is no guarantee of success. But it is difficult to be successful without three skills that I have come to view as imperative: the ability to maintain composure, to facilitate meetings and to communicate well. An abundance of books, articles, tapes and courses provide useful guidance to aspiring leaders. Still, most of them place surprisingly little importance on honing these three imperative competencies. Universally important, they transcend the types of circumstances addressed in theories of leadership or management style, including situational leadership, that are based on the solid principle that what works in one situation may not work in another. The essential skills are the ability to maintain composure, communicate well in public, and facilitate meetings effectively. Any leaders lacking in these three abilities, no matter how skilled they may be in other ways, will find themselves at a huge disadvantage.

IMPERATIVE ONE
WHAT'S REALLY LOST WHEN YOU LOSE IT

An otherwise gifted merchandising executive in a national retailer was famous for tirades in which he would verbally attack his subordinates, railing about how dumb, thoughtless and unmotivated they were. These tirades occurred with sufficient frequency that his subordinates learned to lower their heads and wait for the explosion to lose force so that the meeting could resume. Over time, people grew hardened to his abusive behavior. They lost respect for him and referred to him by several contemptuous nicknames. The executive, though a brilliant man, never achieved his expected degree of career success.

Losing emotional control can be suicidal to the success of any leader. I am referring to a loss of composure which occurs when someone becomes very angry in the presence of others and loses control over how that anger is expressed. Such outbursts invariably surprise and baffle the people who are present, though they may secretly delight those not favorably disposed to the person who has "lost it." When senior people lose composure, others question their basic emotional strength and stability, raising significant doubts about their fitness as leaders.

This seems self-evident. However, in more than 30 years of organizational life I have never heard of anyone being formally coached in the importance of maintaining composure. Leaders may sense it is wrong to "blow their cool," but not know *how* wrong.

BLOWING ONE'S COOL VS. STRATEGIC ANGER

Unlike leaders whose anger results in a loss of composure, those who express anger strategically are very much in control. They draw strength from their anger. By expressing it consciously and with forethought, they use it to their best advantage.

I know of one chief operating officer who employs strategic anger when attacks are being made not at him but at other members of his team. Years ago I received a lesson in strategic anger when I was negotiating with a veteran Teamsters Union president. During some preliminary discussions at one bargaining session, I made a mild and quite innocent joke about whether bargaining unit members would be working very hard as they awaited the results of the negotiations. The union leader immediately turned on me and delivered a stinging diatribe on my treating the interests of working people as a joke. This was, of course, part of his stock in trade as a senior bargainer, but as a relatively inexperienced negotiator it blew me away. I could do nothing other than call a break to regain my composure. As painful as the experience was, trying to fight back in the circumstances would have been more painful.

DEVELOP COPING STRATEGIES

Leaders cannot flourish if they have thin skin. It is a devastating handicap in the cut and thrust of modern organization life. It is possible to grow thicker skin without becoming too calloused. We all need to adopt the little devices and techniques that work for us. The important point to remember is how destructive losing composure really is. Fortunately, maintaining composure grows easier with age. But it would be a lot easier still if management educators, mentors and advisors placed greater emphasis on this subject in their work with clients.

Frequently, when you feel the anger rising, as it inevitably will, the best approach is to bite your tongue and say as little as possible. Sometimes the situation does not permit this. In that case, allow yourself a brief mental "time-out" in order to regain control, and then continue in what others will perceive as a normal tone.

If your anger is aroused by someone's rudeness, then learn how to control your reaction to the insult. It is always sobering to discover how often onlookers don't even realize that an offense has taken place. Often, it is only when we respond in kind that others become aware that there is an issue at all.

A commonly encountered situation is one in which we think our colleagues are not making the required effort. While it is quite appropriate to inquire as to whether our understanding of the situation is correct, it rarely helps to blow a gasket. Frustration is part and parcel of working with others, and it can be another source of anger, especially in situations where we don't have *full* control. Ironically, the result is that by giving in to anger, we lose what limited control we have. There is a great deal of truth in the adage that we attract what we most fear.

Sometimes personalities can cause frustration. I remember how irritating I found one particular member of a team I was leading in a client organization. We worked together over several months and those of us who were involved found several of his mannerisms difficult to bear. I learned that my most effective coping strategy was to repeat a mantra as I walked into that office building. I forced myself to stop in the foyer for a few seconds and repeat to myself, "I will not rise, I will not rise, I will not rise." By and large it worked, and when I bumped into that person years later, I realized that he had no conception of how irritating I had found him.

In spite of our best efforts, we will fall short of perfection. Even though I know perfectly well how damaging it can be to lose composure, I did so myself just a few months ago. I was unexpectedly confronted with a crisis of conscience at a sub-committee meeting of a board on which I sit. I objected strongly to the conditions under which I had been invited to join the sub-committee. Because I regarded those conditions as an intolerable violation of a key governance principle, I felt that I had to take a strong stand on principle and leave the meeting. However, I had not allowed myself adequate time to reflect. Consequently, my explanation to the committee as to why I felt I had to take such extreme measures was poorly delivered. It succeeded only in confusing them. I must admit that my actions, though prompted by a strong belief in the principle, were partly driven by a loss of composure. As is so often the case, I was the prime victim of the incident. It cost me the loss of support of the people who were present.

Threats to our emotional control may diminish with experience, but we can never expect to be entirely free of them. There is no easy way to learn how to maintain control when circumstances threaten to trigger an emotional response, although awareness can help. I find self-reminders useful when I am facing situations I expect to be annoying or offensive, but it is impossible to anticipate every situation. Everyone has an Achilles heel.

PICKING UP THE PIECES

What can we do when we've allowed our strong feelings to overrule our better judgment, and we've lost composure? My friend, Etta Wharton, points out that our organizational conditioning usually teaches us to deny that we have been emotional, so we may find ourselves going to great lengths to justify and explain our irrational behavior in rational terms. Sometimes the situation requires a straightforward acknowledgment that we have had an emotional response to the situation, with a brief explanation as to why. When our strong feelings were directed at an individual, a private discussion might help clear the air. The problem with this is that, while we might be sorry for having lost composure, we are still disapproving of the other person's behavior. In this case, it may be difficult to apologize for our response without retracting our disapproval. It is useful to keep in mind that strong emotions do tend to abate quite quickly. If possible, we should allow ourselves the time to recover and reflect as to whether or not we have done serious damage.

The key principle in picking up the pieces after an emotional outburst is to be honest with yourself, acknowledge that you did lose control, and that your behavior was not effective. What you choose to do about it depends on the specific situation and politics. Your instincts will be the best guide.

IMPERATIVE TWO
LEADING WITH BOTH FEET IN YOUR MOUTH

Most people are well aware that the ability to communicate effectively to an audience is an important skill. So why does this subject receive so little emphasis in management training and education? Some people have a natural flair and they communicate comfortably and fluently. Others hate public speaking and will go to tremendous lengths to avoid it. Some leaders manage to succeed in spite of their awkwardness at presentations and public debates, but they are the exceptions. Some have learned to be reasonably effective, but still hate that aspect of organizational life.

The real price of weak presentation skills must also take into account the hidden costs. People who feel hesitant will avoid speaking at a meeting. Consequently, their contribution is limited. A subtle side-effect is that people who are too timid to enter a group discussion often make up for it later by privately criticizing those who did participate in the discussion. I don't know why we sometimes express our frustrations and our disappointment in ourselves in the form of criticism of others, but this phenomenon is readily apparent. To that extent, the absence of presentation skills harms not only the individual, but the entire group.

Similarly, people who are uncomfortable speaking to a group will not place themselves in a position where they have to make a presentation. Since leadership naturally falls to those who have demonstrated their competence and confidence to others, those who don't speak up are not selected for responsibilities they may be quite competent to carry.

A lack of comfort in a public situation can be even physically dangerous. Many years ago, as a newly appointed member of the executive team of Eaton's, British Columbia and Alberta, I was handed a task that made me very uncomfortable. When honoring employees on their 25- and 40-year service anniversaries, I was the executive most frequently selected to pin the corsages on the dresses of the long service women, many of whom were more than twice my age. You can imagine the consequences of my lack of skill in the delicate operation of getting the pin into the dress but not the person! I was only slightly better at the task of reading the congratulatory letter from the president, John David Eaton. But at least that task didn't put anyone at physical risk. I suspect that part of my discomfort in the situation stemmed from my sense that I was really too young to be involved in a ceremony that was so important to the people being honored.

Occasionally, nervousness in a public speaking situation can be turned to an advantage. When Meryl Manto was a district manager at Beaver Lumber, he was terrified at the prospect of delivering his part of a presentation to a group that included Jim Black, former president of the Molson Companies which owned Beaver Lumber at the time. When Manto's turn came, he rose to his feet and confessed that he'd been so nervous the night before, in anticipation of the meeting, that he couldn't sleep. So he decided to go into the office early for some extra preparation. He shaved, showered, put on his best business suit and arrived at the office at 6:30 that morning only to discover that in his nervousness, he had forgotten to shave one half of his face. Having to turn around and drive home helped relax him.

His story broke up the meeting. Not only was it well told, but it obviously struck a familiar chord among everyone in the room. Most of us have had our own Meryl Manto-like experiences on the road to whatever level of presentation competence we have managed to acquire.

CHAIRING AND FACILITATING MEETINGS

Technology is changing the number and kinds of meetings that people attend. Today we have teleconferencing, e-mail and video conferencing in addition to face-to-face meetings. As video conferencing in particular becomes more affordable, it will reduce the need for business travel. But technology-driven innovations will never completely replace the face-to-face meeting. There will always be a need for people to get together in the same room and do business with one another. Leaders who cannot run an effective meeting will always find themselves at a significant disadvantage since this represents one of the cornerstone competencies.

One of my first bosses at Eaton's used to chair weekly management meetings—the most efficient management meetings I have ever attended. But it would be far more accurate to call them briefings. He would prepare the minutes of the meetings in advance. Then he would read aloud the minutes on each agenda item, ask if anyone had any questions, and move on to the next item. We soon learned that questions were not very welcome!

Such a highly leader-centered style would be ludicrous today, where people who facilitate meetings go to great lengths to draw out thoughts and suggestions from all participants.

TIME SPENT PREPARING FOR MEETINGS IS TIME WELL SPENT

Now that the command-and-control style of leadership has given way to a more consultative approach, facilitation skills have become more relevant. And chief among them is the need for preparation. Now it is even more important to develop an agenda, allocate a time limit to each item and make sure that the discussion stays on track. Poorly run meetings show a supreme disrespect for the value of the participants' time. Everybody in today's organizations is busy. Everybody feels stretched to the limit. Meetings that are not well planned and well run will inevitably cause resentment among those who are required to attend. In fact, there is such growing resistance to the amount of time spent in meetings that many people profess to hate all meetings.

Meeting planning is too often characterized by a high degree of wishful thinking. Items requiring real thought and substantive discussion are allocated no more than a few minutes because the meeting planner hoped that they would not take longer. Participants aren't consulted about whether the items they want are on the agenda. Or they fail to respond to such information ahead of time, so that when people arrive at the meeting, a number of unexpected items are raised for discussion. When people come to meetings unprepared, there is a risk that items will be resolved without adequate information. Alternatively, such items may be tabled until the required information is gathered, causing unnecessary delays.

STAY ON TRACK

The failure to keep discussion on track is one of the areas of greatest complaints among meeting participants. Leading effective discussions is a highly developed art that involves a number of competencies, such as (a) knowing how to test for a consensus; (b) reminding speakers of the topic under discussion; and (c) bringing closure to discussions. These are all skills that improve with practice. Their absence results in prolonged, repetitive discussions that rarely achieve any useful outcome.

FACILITATE = MAKE EASY

The word "facilitate" is related to the French word *facile*, which means "easy." If you check out the word "facilitate" in Microsoft Word's thesaurus, you'll find "to make easy" at the top of the list. Although facilitation skills are similar to those involved in chairing a meeting, they differ in significant ways. In facilitation, the challenge is to enable effective discussion and consensus building without formal position authority. Facilitation reflects some distinct values. The facilitator is expected to maintain neutrality with respect to the issues involved, ensure that all participants are treated as having equal value and draw out all of the participants in the discussion. The goal is to bring the group to a consensus, whether that is expressed in terms of a plan, an action, or a position on the discussion question.

Facilitation skills are highly consistent with the prevailing management paradigm in which people are consulted and expected to contribute to decisions. The leader's role as facilitator enables the new approach to leadership to be fulfilled effectively. It is possible to be an effective leader without being a skilled facilitator, but facilitation skills make for more effective leaders.

Even skilled facilitators may decide to ask someone else to facilitate a discussion in certain circumstances. If, for example, the leader wishes to actively participate in the discussion, or, alternatively, if the leader does not want his or her personal influence to affect the outcome, then it would be wise to appoint someone else to act as the facilitator. When a meeting is facilitated by someone other than the leader, it is important for the leader to cooperate fully with the facilitator and to participate on the same basis as everyone else. Little can be done about the fact that the leader's ideas are likely to hold greater weight than others, but effective facilitation can occur only if the leader shows respect for the facilitator and is willing to follow the facilitator's lead.

Facilitation skills can be learned. When the U.S. business unit of a Canadian-based financial services company underwent an organization transformation process, the members of the management group (which numbered more than 100) were required to spend much of their time in meetings. Several cross-functional teams were busy developing the business systems used to deliver client service, and other teams were involved in developing long- and short-range plans. Realizing that they were spending more time in meetings than not, and that the meetings were not as effective as they needed to be, the executive team developed a model for the management meetings.

The model delineated three roles for the conduct of meetings. The first order of business would be to clarify the roles of chair, facilitator and scribe. Although occasionally two of these roles were combined, the model favored the three separate roles being played by three different people. The model required an agenda to be delivered to all participants 48 hours prior to the meeting, and also required that a meeting objective and planned outcome be identified. The scribe was responsible for creating a written record of all agreed-upon decisions and actions, noting who was responsible for each action and the deadlines for completion. This model was quite conventional, with the possible exception of the delineation of the three separate roles.

All managers were asked to attend a training session to become familiar with the model. The session included basic information for chairs, facilitators and scribes. This simple investment paid healthy dividends. Because of their desire to increase the effectiveness of the time spent at meetings, people were highly motivated to learn the language and follow the guidelines. The model allowed teams to organize and focus their attack on problems, and to have some fun in the process. The ranking participant was not always the one who was delegated as chair or facilitator. Even very senior people took their turns at being scribe, the least desirable of the roles. Executives accepted their assignments with good humor, and the quality of meeting time increased dramatically. The results were surprising, given the simplicity of the approach.

However, the open acknowledgment of the problem and the shared commitment to addressing it did much to stimulate the improvement.

IMPERATIVE THREE
STRATEGIES TO DEVELOP PRESENTATION SKILLS

1. **Make a personal commitment.**

Being an effective presenter is a skill that is not only vital to success but also one that greatly increases the enjoyment of working life. But it doesn't happen by magic. The first step is to acknowledge its importance and develop a personal plan to become better than average. Being ignored, having no influence and being compelled to follow the dictates of others who are no smarter or worthier make for a heavy burden compared to the relatively minor discomfort of developing presentation skills. And the spin-off is greater self-confidence, greater charisma, and increased energy.

2. **Hire a coach.**

My own turnaround came when I had to make a formal presentation to all of the suppliers at Beaver Lumber. It was vital that I do so competently, and I was offered the services of a communications consultant, Bev Dales, who had coached other Molson and Beaver executives. I had been skeptical of the value of this kind of coaching, but I was wrong. Bev is a highly skilled consultant who not only helped me prepare my presentation, but insisted that I practice it repeatedly in front of a video camera. The success of the presentation whetted my appetite to find more opportunities to present and facilitate. My partner, Adrian Palmer, also wanted to move from being an adequate presenter to an excellent presenter. He also hired a coach and within weeks experienced a significant breakthrough in his effectiveness (and therefore his enjoyment) of presentations.

3. **Learn how to answer challenging questions in a public setting.**

The skills required to answer tough, and sometimes hostile, questions in public are not the same as those required to make successful presentations. Senior people in organizations are increasingly expected to meet with groups who have different or conflicting objectives. They need to be trained in how to answer awkward questions convincingly. Most political leaders receive extensive training in precisely this skill, and it would definitely be worthwhile for leaders of non-political organizations to do the same.

4. **Stress the importance of presentation skills in management education programs.**

Some programs already do this, but many do not. This omission in management education curricula is unforgivable and needs to be corrected. The same is true of managerial development programs in larger organizations.

5. **Seek opportunities to build presentation skills through volunteerism.**

Practicing presentation skills within your organization may be practically and psychologically unrealistic. But involvement as a volunteer in the not-for-profit sector offers the opportunity to become involved in presentations and large group discussions in an atmosphere that minimizes career risks. People who become board members and officers gain valuable experience speaking to the media, to government and to various stakeholder groups in a manner not often afforded by their day-to-day working lives.

6. **Take steps to ensure that all managers and executives are skilled at chairing and facilitating meetings.**

No matter how much we may dislike them, meetings are an inescapable part of organization life. The goal is to eliminate the "waste of time" factor by making them as effective, productive and enjoyable as possible. If meetings result in clear decisions on the next steps to be taken, and those steps are followed up, the participants are more likely to feel that their time has been well spent. It helps if the number of meetings can be reduced and their duration shortened. This can be accomplished in part by a rigorous examination of how the organization uses meetings, so that some can be eliminated, others shortened, and others combined. But the best results will come from improving the skills of meeting chairs and facilitators.

7. **Be authentic.**

Authenticity is a subtle quality that inspires confidence and respect among colleagues. It is present in those individuals whose internal sense of self is consistent with the image that they project to others. They have substance. We know that they're made of "the right stuff."

One of the quickest ways to undermine authenticity is to be pompous. There is no question that it takes a certain amount of ego and self-importance to rise to the top, but one of the most devastating errors any leader can make is to demonstrate an excessive sense of self-importance. One president I know frequently refers to himself as "The President," and often prefaces remarks with the phrase, "as President..." People are well aware of who the formal leader is—there is no need for him to point it out. I happen to know this president well enough to know that he is innocent of the attitudes he seems to portray. It is unfortunate that he did not receive coaching at an earlier stage in his career. People find self-importance very annoying, especially in their leaders. Although it's important to take your work very seriously, it's equally important to take yourself not quite as seriously.

CHAPTER 9

BUILD IT AND THEY WILL STAY

"It's not much fun anymore."

These words, spoken by a senior human resource executive, reflect a prevailing experience of the contemporary workplace. People who have survived the changes sweeping most organizations have probably done so because of their talent and adaptability, as well as a little good luck. Most have been profoundly changed by what they have undergone and they may have several contradictory feelings about their experiences. While they may welcome many aspects of the transformed working environment, such as its pace, clearer focus and sense of individual ownership, they may also miss the camaraderie they enjoyed with people who are no longer there. While they may readily agree that their organization is healthier and more able to withstand the rigors of future change, they may still yearn for what they remember as a more stable and predictable working world. The need to constantly meet the demands of others—customers, co-workers and other departments—can be an oppressive burden.

If what we have created is so much better, why doesn't it feel that way? Fortunately, this gloomy picture of the motivational landscape is only one side of the coin. The changes that have occurred in working life can be enjoyable and fulfilling. People feel both the exhilaration and the pressure, with one or the other predominating at any given point in time. We have created a very different working environment, partly by design, partly by accident. It demands a great a deal of people, and therefore, a great deal of the organization in terms of understanding, support and guidance.

A GOOD WORKING ENVIRONMENT IS GOOD BUSINESS

An organization's working environment evolves over time and reflects a unique mix of many factors, including history, the nature of the organization's business, the nature of the workforce and culture. It is rare for the working environment to be seen as an important subject in its own right; something which can be designed to reflect the operational and social needs of people.

When people talk about the working environment, they often are referring to different things. Some people define it within fairly small parameters comprised of the physical setting of the work, the facilities and equipment used and the comfort of the physical environment. Others have a broader concept; one which goes beyond the physical environment to include the organization's culture, working relationships, the nature of the business, employment policies and the kind of work to be done. The broader definition is more helpful because it includes more factors that affect the level of performance an organization can achieve.

It makes good sense to consciously develop a clear picture of the distinctive working environment best suited to your organization and its people. Once that is clarified, it is also important to develop the environment so that it is in alignment with the strategic direction of the organization. But for this to be productive, leaders must first overcome their cynicism about people's motivation in focusing on the working environment.

This lesson was brought home to me recently when I worked with a team charged with developing recommendations to improve the working environment in a not-for-profit organization. Some of the administrative staff felt very strongly that their workstations had been designed and located in a highly distracting manner. Each of the three floors of the administrative headquarters was physically divided by an aisle which went from the reception area through half of the floor directly to some private offices. This aisle cut right through the middle of some secretarial work stations. Naturally, as people moved through the aisle, they stopped to chat with the administrative staff in the open workstations. As you can imagine, this proved to be extremely distracting, causing continual interruptions and lack of privacy. When the team presented their recommendations, including a proposal to redesign the workstations, senior management reacted negatively. Their concern was that the recommendation involved a fairly significant cost, especially since they perceived the underlying motivation to be frivolous and self-interested. I argued, to no avail, that the underlying motivation was constructive. In their efforts to explain the decision not to approve the recommendation, senior management unintentionally offended team members which caused the situation to heat up to disastrous degrees. The incident, which said a great deal about that particular organization's history, illustrates that systematic attention to the working environment may still be considered a frill.

Office technology is an increasingly important part of the working environment and it warrants serious attention. As we all are well aware, breakthroughs in applying information technology to office work have been revolutionary. These changes have created the situation where every individual has an immense impact on the organization. As people and technology become more closely integrated, investing in the right environment becomes more important and the issue less trivial.

As we gain more experience of transformed organizations, we better understand the impact they have on the people who work within them. Whether such organizations are experienced positively or negatively depends on the individual organization and such factors as whether it is growing, has already undergone significant change, is using new or old technology, and is comprised of skilled staff. The motivational landscape has been shifting, and the extent to which people are achieving fulfillment of their psychological needs remains an open question. But one thing is certain: the idea that an organization should carefully craft its own working environment is gaining importance. There is growing recognition that an organization's intellectual capital is not only a valuable asset, but possibly the key asset which differentiates its level of performance and success. The ability to create an environment in which people can flourish is not only possible, it is a legitimate strategic tool in its own right. But it must be built on an accurate, dispassionate understanding of what people really care about and what aspects of their working lives they find disturbing.

THE MOTIVATIONAL LANDSCAPE

EMPLOYEES' NEEDS AND MOTIVES

Is it realistic to expect leaders to accommodate all the needs and motives operating at any given time? Perhaps not. But they have to appreciate the *complexity* of all the factors that combine to motivate their people. It's so easy to oversimplify and misunderstand the underlying psychological motives of even their closest associates. It's not at all uncommon to find conflicting motives, or breathtakingly rapid change in what's important in a given situation.

All of the following motives may be relevant at any time:

- *Security*—the certainty that employment will continue.

- *Stability*—a return to an environment of relatively little change, or even to the "good old days" where things are like they used to be.

- *Voice*—some real influence and control.
- *Respect, understanding and support.*
- *Leadership*—that can be respectful and trusted.
- *Opportunity*—for career growth and advancement.
- *Meaning*—some elevating social value to the work or the organization's contribution to a cause.
- *A payoff*—fair and appropriate financial reward.
- *Interesting work*—a balance between challenge and the ability to accomplish.

These motives, operating in most working environments, may not be obvious. People learn to hide their feelings if they believe that forthright communication would be damaging. For this reason, even leaders who take pride in being in touch with employee attitudes and morale, will find it useful to check their assumptions before undertaking decisions that will affect people.

EMPLOYMENT SECURITY

People have learned to be circumspect in the way they express their fears and aspirations. Few organizations have managed to avoid their own brand of political correctness. Everyone understands that there are certain things you don't say if you want to be regarded as part of the organization's future. Nevertheless, when you look at confidential employment surveys in a variety of organizations and when you speak to employees when they are feeling safe and relaxed, if they ever are feeling relaxed these days, their dominant concern continues to be employment security. This is often the case even where there is no rational basis for concern. Most of us have felt the effects of organizational downsizing, either personally or vicariously, through the experience of family members or friends. The trauma is horrible, something we want to avoid at all costs. The prospect of losing a job really does strike fear into our hearts and it is difficult to ever completely put the fear aside. The fact that we may be talented and highly capable is no longer a guarantee that it won't happen to us. So naturally, we tend to interpret what we witness in organization life with exaggerated concern. But we can't show our concern for fear of appearing paranoid or lacking in confidence, or even worse—negative. This is why senior executives are often taken aback when told about lingering employment anxiety in their organization: its manifestations are so carefully concealed.

Employment-related anxiety has many effects. With all the unemployed, highly educated, highly motivated recent graduates crowding the labor market, current employees feel easily replaceable. People are reluctant to voice criticism of initiatives about which they have reservations lest they be seen as nay-sayers or critics. They may feel they have no choice but to work hard supporting directions whose validity they do not accept. They may find it difficult to trust and be open with their leaders who hold life-and-death control over their future. No matter how hard they try, most people can't count on promotions anymore. "The climb up the corporate ladder is becoming more difficult and more precarious. All the hard work was somehow more acceptable when it led to promotion and the rewards that went with it. Now it is a matter of struggling to hang on to what you have already achieved."[1]

The transition from the old psychology of entitlement is still proving to be difficult for many people.[2] The psychology of entitlement is a useful concept which helps explain one of the most profound changes in the motivational landscape. Employees are generally aware they cannot depend on their employers to fulfill as many of their needs as they once did. Breaking the chain of dependency is economically necessary and probably psychologically desirable but nevertheless a very painful process. The resulting sense of having lost something of value feeds any negative feelings about the new working environment. As in most organization changes, it's a matter of two steps forward, one step back.

A QUESTION OF LOYALTY

We still hear the occasional executive deplore the lack of loyalty on the part of employees. The expectation that employees be loyal has always been a little difficult to understand since the essence of the employer/employee contract has been a *quid pro quo*, certainly economic, and social and psychological as well. It's obvious that the contract has been changing in the wake of dismissals and layoffs. When senior people talk about the psychology of entitlement and tell employees that they must be less dependent on the organization, then all bets are off. Loyalty has become a word that now evokes nostalgia or anger.

---

[1] "Healing the Wounds," by David M. Noer, Jossey Boss Inc. 1993.

[2] For a thought-provoking analysis of the dangers of entitlement in the workplace, see *Danger in the Comfort Zone*, by Judith M. Bardwick, American Management Association, 1991.

Actually, the notion of loyalty has always been prone to misunderstanding. Executives imagine that employees owe loyalty in return for their livelihood. In that context, for example, for employees to join a union would be perceived as an act of disloyalty. Employees, on the other hand, talk about "giving all those years" to the employer, as if it were an act of great self sacrifice and altruism. This concept of loyalty is really an anachronism and neither party should expect it of the other.

There are growing indications that the new workforce takes a totally different attitude to work and working relationships. In "The Decline of Deference," Neil Nevitte analyses the trend to "post-material" values, including the decline in respect for authority. He asks, "How do you renew confidence in leaders and institutions and restore the depleted reservoirs of trust? And how to reverse a deeper slide into cynicism?"[3]

When people in organizations refer to the "suits," we know who they're talking about. And there is scant respect in the characterization. In private, and increasingly in public, the new work force is likely to treat what they perceive as the puffed-up, self-important behavior of executives with brutal disdain. Some older executives are having difficulty adjusting to an environment in which other people don't automatically defer to them. Some senior executives are particularly prone to developing what I call the "executive view of life": over time, they begin to perceive other parts of the economic system, particularly government and the not-for-profit sector, as not only inferior in value and talent, but as inimical to their interests.

While most executives and managers have adapted surprisingly easily to the more egalitarian style of relationships, some are resistant, firm in their belief that we will eventually regain our respect for authority. Whether or not that happens, senior people in organizations need to learn how to "go with the flow" and develop greater comfort with being strongly challenged personally and professionally by the new and less reverent employee. It can be unnerving for one's most sincere and straightforward communication to be treated with cynicism and disbelief. But that is increasingly a feature of organizational life. It goes without saying that executives need to learn not to rise to the tide of their own frustrations but rather to steer a steady course of calmly setting out the facts as they understand them.

---

[3] "The Decline of Defense," by Neil Nevitte, Broadview Press, 1996.

THE LACK OF SLACK

In the early '90s, Mary Baetz and I researched the impact on people of the changes then sweeping the workplace. As we talked to senior managers from business, government and the not-for-profit sectors, we gradually became aware of a phenomenon we called the "Lack of Slack."[4] We defined it as the chronic state of having more to do than can be done in the time available. The phenomenon is not entirely new but it has developed in recent years with such intensity that it now seems almost universal. Most of our work was done between 1990 and 1992. Since then, the forces causing Lack of Slack have developed further and there is wider recognition that the demands on people may not be sustainable in the long term. Mary and I were struck by how often people would exclaim, "You are describing my life!" when we explained the Lack of Slack.

We encountered a few managers and executives whose response was quite unsympathetic. To them, the Lack of Slack was a necessary development and a small price to pay for improved organizational effectiveness and competitiveness. They were inclined to suggest that people, in the words of one participant, "should stop whining and get on with the job." While there is probably a kernel of wisdom in this reaction, it misses the point. It is clear that sustained frenzy is destructive for many, perhaps most, people. Some years ago, *Fortune Magazine* ran a long series of articles on the adverse effects and organizational costs of stress and burnout. Some of these articles documented a growing trend towards the *flight* of talented people away from organizational life to other, less destructive careers.

CAUSES OF THE LACK OF SLACK

What are the factors that have led us to this unintended place? Ironically, the Lack of Slack is an outcome of organization changes which have been very positive, such as streamlining, more competitive, customer-oriented structures and more efficient operations. For that reason, it is unrealistic to think that the pace of organizational life will slow much, if at all. At the same time, the Lack of Slack can be stimulating, even exhilarating.

I still encounter many people who are so anxious and uncertain about employment security, that they do everything they can to keep their heads down so they won't be noticed in the next round of downsizing. When executives talk about the need to adapt to a climate of perpetual change and restruc-

---

[4] "Does Your Organization Have a Lack of Slack?" *Western Management Consultants Newsletter,* November 1991.

turing, employees may find the prospect exhausting and even terrifying. The strain of learning new technology, particularly computer technology, is obvious. Less obvious, but equally demanding, are the costs of learning new attitudes and behaviors. It can be difficult for people to accept that "the customer is always right" when they experience the abuse that anyone in a customer interface role inevitably encounters. It can even be argued that the proliferation of labor-saving technology, such as car phones, fax machines and voice mail, contribute to the pressures of our working days. They demand our immediate response, no matter where we are or what we are doing. Similarly, in terms of labor savings, information technology may not be all that it is cracked up to be. Participants in our focus groups ruefully acknowledged that most computer systems projects they knew about did not produce labor savings for those involved in either the implementation or ongoing management of the system.

Another cause relates to the style of open communication and consultation. Group problem solving and teamwork take time and invariably involve meetings of one kind or another. It would be impossible to prove quantitatively that people are spending more time in meetings these days, but few people doubt it. The problem, as everyone knows only too well, is that while the meetings go on, work back at the office continues to pile up, creating a state of perpetual anxiety.

The frenetic pace characterized by the Lack of Slack has given rise to many casualties, of which the greatest is planning. Discussions about the importance of planning are likely to arouse cynicism. During our focus group discussions, one manager made the poignant comment that he was no longer able to meet his own quality standards since there simply wasn't time to do so.

FOCUS ON INTERNAL FACTORS

Because it results from the way other forces and factors interact, the Lack of Slack does not lend itself easily to a direct solution. You can hardly reduce employee stress by deciding to back off from a commitment to quality customer service. Adding more staff does not always reduce the workload of current staff since they often become responsible for training, monitoring and dealing with the consequences of mistakes new people tend to make. Some organizations try to ameliorate the effects by introducing fitness centers, workplace exercise programs and even coffee klatch spaces in the middle of the work area. Measures such as these probably help, but fail to tackle the underlying causes.

A more fruitful approach is to distinguish between any external and environmental factors which have led to the Lack of Slack, and those which are internal. Presumably, it is more possible to influence the latter. Organizations, like people, fall into various habits and ways of thinking. Sometimes, there is a kind of macho attitude involved, with people competing to be seen as the busiest or the hardest working. In professional service firms, there is often a direct relation between hours worked or billed and internal status, with the highest billers being the most influential. Executives may communicate directly or indirectly that they place value on long hours, weekend work and other manifestations of corporate commitment. In a survey we conducted of 112 organizations, 28 percent of the respondents believed that senior management would not be very concerned about the Lack of Slack in their organizations. Thankfully, 52 percent of responding organizations believed that their senior managers *would* be concerned. [5]

The expectations and behavior of senior managers is central to whether or not people will feel encouraged to achieve a balance between working and personal lives. The CEO who encourages people to seek balanced lives while scheduling 7:30 a.m. or 5:00 p.m. management meetings demonstrates what he or she really feels is important.

FLEXIBLE WORKING ARRANGEMENTS

Flexible working arrangements present one of the most promising directions in helping people achieve better balance between work and home. Until recently, there has been a great deal more said than done about such arrangements, particularly work sharing and working at home. Admittedly, there are real impediments to both approaches. Work sharing is extremely difficult to accommodate within the constraints of current employment legislation and employee benefits plans. Although the concept of work sharing has been around for a while, few qualified people appear to be interested in adopting it. Working at home also presents potential difficulties, such as the cost of providing people with computer equipment and systems that work from remote sites. Even though they would be reluctant to say so publicly, many managers worry that working-at-home arrangements would be abused, since such work would be unsupervised.

---

[5] "Lack of Slack—Survey Results," *Western Management Consultants Newsletter,* May 1992.

STRATEGIES TO MAKE THE WORKING ENVIRONMENT AN ASSET

Addressing the changing motivational landscape and the increasing Lack of Slack are major considerations in the creation of a productive working environment. A comprehensive strategy to create the environment that works best for the organization will be an area of considerable focus in the future. Any planned approach to creating a positive working environment should include the following six considerations.

1. **Keep in touch with employee attitudes.**

Use of employee attitude or climate surveys has been at a high level during recent years. Many organizations conduct such surveys yearly. Some surveys are designed to function as baseline studies so that year-to-year changes can be monitored and responded to. Other organizations use outside survey services so that they can compare their results with those of other companies in the outside supplier's database. Whether surveys are conducted internally or externally, it's a good idea to track changes in attitudes to glean information that helps guide senior management.

However, there are also some well-known drawbacks to employee attitude surveys, with the most significant being that they set up the expectation of a response, an expectation that organizations may or may not be able to meet. Moreover, people are becoming survey weary, with the result that it becomes difficult to maintain adequate levels of staff participation. Still, surveys provide the kind of quantitative data and rational analysis that managers and executives respect. Other methods of keeping in touch with employees include employee advisory committees, focus groups and suggestion plans, all of which have a useful role in staying in touch with employees.

I recently helped the executive director of a large seniors' services organization interpret the results of the first employee attitude survey that organization had ever conducted. The results fell within normal expected ranges. There were plenty of areas in which employees were strongly supportive, such as the organization's overall direction, the professionalism of management and employee pride in both the organization and the work. At the same time, employees were sharply critical of two areas: compensation practice and management's openness to new ideas. These messages, particularly the latter, were difficult for management to hear. But the results were completely clear and statistically powerful. Working with the board of directors and the human resources committee, the executive director was able to develop concrete plans to address the areas of employee dissatisfaction. So, in this organization, the survey proved most helpful. It pointed management's attention to the real problems and allowed limited staff resources to be allocated to the highest priority issues. In acknowledging, at an all-staff meeting, the messages inherent in the results of the survey, the executive director added to her credibility as a leader and the staff felt valued by her response. Many organizations have had similarly positive experiences with surveys. It's interesting that such an old management tool has sustained acceptance over such a long period of time and, if anything, is better suited to the needs of the current organization context than when the technique was first introduced.

2. Keep the dialogue going.

As useful as these techniques may be, they cannot replace the value of ongoing dialogue with the leaders. Our emerging concepts of organizational leadership increasingly position the leader at the center of communication. This is a particularly challenging expectation considering that so often the resulting dialogue is very difficult. On the one hand, some of the attitudes and assumptions expressed by leaders seem to employees to be far removed from their day-to-day experience. On the other hand, employees may have expectations of leaders that go far beyond any reasonable prospect of being fulfilled.

It can be tempting to give up, especially when people are rude and disrespectful. In huge organizations, the logistics often make face-to-face dialogue impossible so that tools such as video tapes and e-mail are required. But somehow, leaders must keep the dialogue going. Once they withdraw from that constant, face-to-face and head-to-head exchange of views, the question and answer and debate, they become dependent on indirect sources of information and other people's interpretation of organizational reality.

Some leaders are masters at this kind of direct communication. Don Cain, a retired corporate president, had a practice of asking employees to write him individual letters expressing their views on important issues. Cain promised that he would get back to them and he always did. Whenever he visited a company location, he would meet with employees at all levels and engage in dialogue about company affairs and issues. Over time, people came to realize that he expected open and challenging discussion and they trusted that their views would be listened to and respected. Some of the discussions were stunningly candid. Employees challenged executive compensation levels and the validity of some of the company's business plans, subjects that were uncomfortable for Cain to deal with, but which kept the dialogue going.

3. Introduce more flexible working arrangements.

It is time to get serious about helping people manage the demands of contemporary life. The fact that there are real impediments to schemes such as work sharing, working at home and contract work, is no reason to give up on them. Employees should be consulted about how to achieve flexible working arrangements. This is a subject that affects them directly and they will have much to contribute in thinking through and solving problems. For example, there is a downside to working at home. It may mean losing contact with co-workers and missing key information about what's going on. When challenged to come up with solutions to problems such as this, people are capable of the most amazing creativity, particularly if they strongly support the goal.

Key suppliers, such as employee benefits carriers, should also be expected to come up with workable solutions for problems that impede innovations such as work sharing. One professional institute worked with their employee benefits consultants to develop a new flexible benefits program which provided employees with a number of optional packages to tailor their coverage to individual requirements.

Attitudinal change may be more difficult to overcome, as in the case of managers who doubt that employees are capable of a sufficient level of self management to work well at home. The truth is that most people in organizations, regardless of level, understand the potential risks and realities. They are usually willing to address them candidly, if asked to be part of developing workable solutions. In the final analysis, it boils down to trust and mature negotiations.

4. Influence behavior through modeling.

Balancing the major components of one's life is something that leaders have to demonstrate as much as possible through their own behavior. If executives routinely stay in the office long after closing time, others will too. If they are unable to relax and enjoy positive relationships with colleagues, the impact on the culture will be profound. If the relationships are competitive, if they manage by crisis, fail to allocate significant time for planning, then others will follow suit.

Modeling behavior is one of the key ways in which leaders influence others. Because people truly believe that actions speak louder than words, they watch very carefully to see what their leaders actually do in practice. If avoiding burnout is to be taken seriously, leaders will show others how to do it, principally through their own actions. Their track records on matters that have to do with humanizing the workplace will be monitored closely.

5. Facilitate professional development.

Concepts like professional development and career-long training tend to attract more talk than action. Yet continuous learning is one of the best means of avoiding burnout and helping people retain a sense of control over their working lives. That is, if the educational expectations are not imposed on top of all the other priorities and workload. The reason why relatively few organizations live up to their own intention statements in the area of professional development is related to the urgency and compelling importance of today's priorities—the Lack of Slack. Training, like planning, has a tendency to fall quickly off the agenda in the face of a crisis or financial crunch. As understandable as this is, the result is a sharp acceleration in the burn-out curve.

One of the more effective approaches is found in large professional firms such as Price Waterhouse Coopers. There, professional staff are required to devote a specified number of working hours per year to individual professional development. Each professional has significant choice in the selection of which course or other educational initiative to participate in. The plan is presented to the firm, approved and tracked within the firm's monthly billing system. A nice balance is achieved between allowing the staff to define and address their own development needs and requiring a minimum level of real development action.

Information technology is an especially important focus for professional development. As consultants, we encounter organizations that have failed to follow up significant investments in technology with education initiatives to help people to use it effectively. Although the labor-saving benefits of information technology may have been overstated, anyone who cannot use technology well will be at a significant disadvantage. In the future, work and technology will become so highly integrated that they will be inseparable. It is generally thought that the older employees are the ones who face the greatest need for adaptation. If so, the problem will disappear in the natural passage of time. But most organizations cannot afford to wait, especially if it is their most experienced, most senior employees who are failing to embrace the technology. Real support and useful training is required. Sending people to an off-site course may be helpful, but they will need support when they return from such a course and face the problem of how to apply the technology in their work. In many organizations, the people responsible for implementing information technology are different from those responsible for education planning, and this can lead to a fragmented approach. Organizations need to come to terms with the education dimensions of introducing information technology effectively.

6. Reduce time spent in meetings.

This is, of course, easier said than done. Otherwise, more organizations would have succeeded in reducing the time spent in meetings. Meetings are not inherently a bad thing; the problem arises from excess—too many meetings, meetings which are too long, or meetings which are just not effective. Each organization must find its own means of reducing the time and energy consumed by meetings.

Some of the more interesting ideas explored in this area include:

- declaring one day per week as a "meetless" day
- using teleconferences to replace face-to-face meetings
- insisting on better preparation for meetings. For example, have one or two people develop the ideas to be discussed before the team invests time in a meeting

FIX IT: IT'S BROKEN

The time has come to recognize the importance of the working environment as a critical business issue. We need to stop treating it as a luxury. The conditions necessary for sustained productivity and staff retention involve more than the obvious tangibles like accommodations and equipment. We need to recognize that working in a positive and respectful setting is not the inappropriate expectation of pampered employees; it is an opportunity to demonstrate the employer's understanding of how hard it is to perform at a consistently high level in most jobs. Those employers who manage the working environment well will reap handsome dividends in the coming competition for the best people.

CHAPTER **10**

CARING ENOUGH TO CONFRONT: HOW TO MANAGE PERFORMANCE AND BEHAVIOR PROBLEMS

Several years ago I was consulting to the management group of one of the business units of a large multi-national. We were engaged in a number of initiatives designed to fundamentally shift the mission, culture and performance of the business. It was a very intense and demanding time for the management group, who were attempting to juggle the imperatives of the change process while sustaining a complex day-to-day operation. In the midst of the process, a middle manager returned from international assignment and was given a special assignment until a more permanent one could be arranged. By virtue of his level and experience, he became part of the change process. He was assigned to a number of the teams and attended the various workshops and communication meetings through which change was being driven. The problem was that he was not highly respected. In fact, over the preceding years, he'd developed a reputation for being lazy and more committed to his individual interests than the needs of the business. The points he made during workshops were perceived to be without much value and his unexplained absences and seemingly low level of effort contributed to the general resentment towards him. It was obvious that he enjoyed little support from colleagues who were openly speculating that he would not survive long in the circumstances.

What I found most striking, however, was that the manager seemed completely unaware of his lack of standing. In my effort to explore the background of the situation, I learned that these problems were long standing and chronic. When I (indirectly) tested his perception of the situation during some casual conversations with him, I learned that he really had no idea whatsoever of the negative way in which he was perceived. It wasn't long before the axe did, in fact, fall and he was terminated. Unable to find work with another organization, he eventually dropped out of sight without ever understanding why his career had ended so unsuccessfully.

Such cases are not isolated. In most organizations there are people who are known to have difficulty in achieving required performance standards or who consistently behave in a way which is fundamentally unacceptable within that culture. But somehow they manage to survive year after year until the underlying difficulties finally come to a crisis and they are terminated, cast adrift into an often unfriendly employment market.

Of all of the organization and leadership challenges addressed in this book, the failure to deal effectively with behavior and performance problems represents the greatest breakdown in the quality of organization functioning. Surely we can do better than to condone and even reinforce performance and behavior which is dysfunctional not only for the organization, but also for the individuals themselves. And surely we can aspire to a situation where correctable performance problems are addressed before they become terminal.

Failure to receive honest feedback can have devastating consequences. After losing his job as a senior planning executive with a major corporation, a friend of mine sought another position and couldn't understand why his search was going so badly. On several occasions he was told that he was the leading candidate, but then experienced a sudden cooling of interest and ultimately was informed that another candidate had been selected. The pattern was so consistent that he wondered whether the problem was negative references. He arranged to meet his former boss and the corporate vice president of human resources, both of whom assured him that the references they were giving were as previously agreed. The situation still didn't make sense, so he asked me to help him out by retaining the services of a company specializing in reference checking, and I agreed to do so.

The report confirmed my friend's worst fears. Both his former superior and the corporate vice president of human resources had given very damaging references, much different from what they had agreed. My friend went back to them, this time armed with the report. The president and human resources vice president were very embarrassed but justified their actions on the basis that they were afraid to tell my friend how they *really* felt about his performance because of their fear of legal liability. A new agreement was struck about future references and my friend ultimately succeeded in finding alternate employment. Thankfully, this kind of unintended damage is relatively rare, but it does illustrate the tendency to pull punches and avoid telling people the truth about their performance.

The reasons why leaders don't do a better job of managing individuals with unproductive attitudes and behavior are, like most of the issues in this book, complex. They involve a variety of interconnected factors that include interpersonal dynamics, leadership style and contemporary social values and attitudes. As Gwendolyn Sedderfield, executive director of a major arts council observed, "Managers are not provided with very good tools or processes to manage individual performance effectively." I have always been struck by how much faith human resource managers place in performance appraisal methodologies which clearly don't work well in many organizations.

RETHINKING PERFORMANCE MANAGEMENT

The traditional performance management model has been evolving for the past 30 years and has changed very little since it was first used in the late sixties. George Odiorne was one of the early theorists who advocated the benefits of "formalized performance appraisal," as it was then called. The model consists of the following well-known steps which can be arranged and communicated in an infinite variety of ways:

1. Performance objectives and targets are set for forthcoming period, typically one year;

2. The individual's success at achieving objectives is appraised periodically, most frequently on an annual basis. Often the appraisee develops a draft for discussion with his or her organizational superior;

3. A performance appraisal interview is conducted by the organizational superior. The individual's success or failure at achieving objectives is discussed together with strengths and weaknesses and, possibly, career development plans;

4. In some systems, rewards for good performance are communicated in the form of salary increases or incentives;

5. Performance objectives and targets for the following period are agreed upon. This step often includes a discussion of individual development or educational plans and career aspirations.

This basic model has been remarkably resilient when you consider how many problems are associated with it. We need to consider why it is that the most seasoned and experienced managers so often avoid completing scheduled performance appraisals. It's not good enough to blame this phenomenon on bad management. But the question remains: if these tools were genuinely helpful, wouldn't we expect them to be embraced by the most experienced managers? It's time we looked at this issue head on.

WEAKNESSES OF TRADITIONAL PERFORMANCE APPRAISALS
FAILURE TO ACCOUNT FOR A CHANGING ENVIRONMENT

There are many reasons why traditional performance appraisals rarely work. To start with, in the face of the tumultuous changes impacting most organizations today, performance objectives can rapidly become obsolete and irrelevant. The performance management system can collapse under the weight of trying to keep up with continuously changing internal and external environments. When people sit down at the end of the performance period to discuss performance, they are likely to find themselves dealing with criteria which both parties know are not as important as they once were or that ignore other considerations which have become even more important than the original objectives. To this extent, the technique of setting performance objectives, which is an integral part of the traditional model, may simply be too static to accommodate our fast-changing world.

DEMOCRATIZATION OF THE WORKPLACE

We must also remember that the performance management model was developed and applied at a time when people generally accepted the boss as the legitimate judge and arbiter of performance. But criticism by authority figures is no longer a widely accepted part of our culture. We no longer grant such authority to anyone. As any teacher, manager, or parent can attest, people are inclined to challenge the validity of any evaluation which is unfavorable to them. It takes a long time before they are ready to consider that the criticism may be valid. We cannot assume that even the most well-intentioned, constructive criticism will be accepted.

This has led people who deliver performance feedback to decide that criticism must be very gentle indeed and balanced with an equal or greater dose of praise. Many human resource professionals and managers fervently believe that feedback should never be critical; that it must be expressed in terms of suggestions or skills development or performance enhancement. The risk is that the message is lost in the process of finding positive words to describe negative behavior or results. The person at the receiving end may not be able to read between the lines to decipher the real message. Being told that you might consider dealing with your colleagues more as if they were clients is not quite the same as being told that your colleagues think you are hell on wheels to deal with.

THE EASY WAY OUT

Many of us are gun shy at delivering negative feedback, especially if we know the reaction will be strongly negative. Experienced managers know that delivering negative feedback, no matter how necessary, can seriously damage important working relationships. It's a small wonder they pull punches in the interest of collegial relationships. In some organization cultures, loyalty to colleagues is very important.

One CEO of a nation-wide business organization knew that two of his vice presidents were locked in a political battle. As the battle intensified, the standard of behavior between the two and their respective teams deteriorated. Enormous energy was consumed in playing out the rivalry and trying to discredit the other side. No one could understand why the president was tolerating such a damaging situation. The answer was that he felt such strong personal loyalty to both of the vice presidents that he felt he had to continue to support them both as part of his unspoken contract with them. To an uninvolved observer, the situation seemed to be based on favoritism; in reality, it was an inappropriate application of the value of loyalty. These are extreme cases, but they demonstrate some of the ways in which systemic factors can impede effective performance feedback.

VICIOUS CIRCLE SYNDROME

If the boss/subordinate relationship is solid, both parties may survive the appraisal interview with their relationship intact. If the relationship is already strained, the negative feedback might be the *coup de grace*. The performance appraisal situation does involve a fundamental inequality in power, which can make receiving negative feedback seem like abuse. In a recent article in the *Harvard Business Review*, Jean François Manzoni and Jean-Louis Barsoux describe the "set-up-to-fail" syndrome[1] in a way that explains what happens when bosses lose confidence in the performance and judgment of their subordinates. The boss typically reacts by supervising more closely. The subordinate resents this, which sets up a vicious circle of psychological withdrawal and defensiveness from which they may never recover. The same thing can happen

---

[1] "The Set-Up-To-Fail Syndrome," by Jean-François Manzoni and Jean-Louis Barsoux, *Harvard Business Review*, March/April, 1998.

in performance feedback meetings when the feedback seems excessively critical. In such cases, the feedback actually leads to a deepening of the performance and relationship problems. Experienced managers know about these risks, which is why they tend to approach appraisal processes with such trepidation. They well understand that the psycho-dynamics of the appraisal meeting are very complex and can lead to mutual misunderstanding and resentment. Like anxious spouses, we don't want to say anything for fear of making it worse.

THE ROLE OF THE CULTURE

Organizational culture can prevent managers from confronting performance and behavior problems. One manager in a large provincial Crown Corporation told me that he definitely softens the message that he delivers during performance appraisal feedback because he doesn't want to develop a reputation as a "hard-ass" in an environment where managers generally don't give negative feedback. His concern is that if he becomes known as an exceptionally tough manager he will not compete well in internal competitions for talented staff. When he confronted an ineffective and disruptive union employee on his staff, he had an experience so common that it seemed apocryphal. The employee filed a grievance which was subsequently "traded off" by the corporate labor relations department as part of an initiative to clear a backlog of grievances. The manager was left with a particularly humiliating defeat in his attempt to confront a legitimate behavioral problem.

LACK OF TRAINING

A little knowledge can be a dangerous thing. New managers might find themselves conducting performance appraisal and feedback interviews with little training in their intricacies, and it may be difficult for them to resist the temptation to duck the tough issues entirely. (The opposite problem is even more serious, where the new supervisor approaches the appraisal as a power trip and an opportunity to play out the new position of authority.)

Even with proper training, performance appraisal methods and tools can be difficult to use. Managers complain that filling the multitude of forms is unnecessarily time consuming and that the benefits do not justify the effort.

EVIDENCE OF PERFORMANCE DEFICIENCY SEEMS SO TRIVIAL

Etta Wharton is an executive with an extensive background in managing cultural diversity. She relates a story involving an employee who failed to win a desired promotion and asked the hiring manager why. The employee was told that she did not have the required communication skills. When asked to inter-vene, Etta asked the manager to detail on what basis it had been determined that the employee's communication skills were deficient. The manager had tremendous difficulty doing so. At last he produced a brief corner note which the employee had attached to her resume. The hand written note included one sentence with a plural noun and a singular verb.

Experienced managers know that their evaluation may be challenged by an employee. Because they don't have time to keep records of everything that occurs, they must rely on their memory and that may consist of no more than a couple of incidents which, when expressed, take on the trivial quality of nit-picking. The problems of evidence and adequate proof can be insurmount-able, particularly if the feedback relates to the person's attitudes or behavior. Consequently, experienced managers may choose to avoid bringing important issues to someone's attention because they know that the evidence to support these issues will seem trivial.

IF PERFORMANCE APPRAISAL IS DESIGNED TO SERVE A MULTIPLICITY OF PURPOSES, IT MAY DO NONE OF THEM VERY WELL

Performance appraisal is often designed to accomplish many objectives:

- to reward performance
- to facilitate employee development
- to provide a basis for compensation decision
- sometimes, to be part of the documentation to be used in connection with discipline or termination

Some applications, however, exclude the use of others. If you want to use the program as a stimulus for staff development, for example, then you shouldn't also use it as the basis for compensation rewards. Staff development is a long-term endeavor, while compensation is more immediate. When people know that the appraisal rating determines their salary increase or bonus, they will perceive performance feedback in that context alone and will pay little attention to any development aspects of the feedback.

When used to provide an important part of a case justifying discipline or termination, performance appraisal may be a particularly *inappropriate* tool. Etta Wharton believes that employees tend to catch on very quickly when a case is being built against them, since the tone and context changes in a subtle but detectable way. Sustaining trust in performance appraisal and feedback is a delicate matter. Employee survey after survey demonstrate that employees regard negative evaluations of their performance as subjective and biased and, if the program is used to help build a case for dismissal, that fear may be quite justified.

Of course, the fact remains that all organizations have to confront the need to terminate people from time to time. Some people are simply not able to meet the performance demands, in spite of their best efforts. It is not always possible to transfer employees to other roles and, in fact, transferring an unsuccessful employee is harmful if the underlying competency issues are not resolved. Some people are unable to change unproductive attitudes and behavior and, ultimately, do need to leave. This is a very troubling reality, particularly for those who have been brought up to believe in the universal possibility of redemption. Firing is the ultimate industrial sanction, and it represents a mutual failure. It is a step some people take with ease, and others cannot take at all. It remains a necessity, provided the organization has done everything reasonable to avoid it.

Very occasionally we find in organizations, as in life, people who are so unredeemingly destructive that their presence poses a threat to the well-being of the organization and the people who work there, and no amount of patience, support or counseling will change their embittered destructiveness. Some managers discuss these rare individuals in terms of "organizational evil." Such people cannot be tolerated. They must be removed.

In fact, performance appraisal systems are not the best places to deal with discipline problems or terminations. Ideally, discipline will be part of a separate process of meetings, measurement and reviews, which must be consistent with the performance appraisal process but separate from it. It's important to have realistic expectations of what performance appraisal systems can do. They are most effective in providing performance feedback as part of a longer-term individual development process. They can't be all things to all people.

TOP LEVEL MANAGERS RARELY PARTICIPATE IN THE ORGANIZATION'S PERFORMANCE MANAGEMENT PROGRAM

I know of no formal study that investigates whether presidents and divisional managers of major organizations use their company's performance management program themselves, but my observation is that they rarely do. This is, of course, a telling comment on the perceived value of such programs. If leaders don't think the techniques are good enough for them, can they be very good for anyone? And why would leaders even passively support programs that they wouldn't use themselves?

When dealing effectively with tough people problems, leaders may also be subject to another influence. Generally, people reserve a greater degree of deference and courtesy for their company's leaders, so senior people may never fully appreciate the magnitude of the behavior problem involved. Behavioral problems which are clearly evident to managers are often less obvious to the leaders. Even when they are aware of the problems, they don't face the same day-to-day frustrations as those faced by the problem employee's co-workers. It's easier for leaders to tolerate offensive behavior because it tends to affect them less directly (and less profoundly) than it does others in the management group. Occasionally, leaders underplay or are dismissive of the problem employee's effect on the others in the organization, as if they have the right to decide for others what is bearable. This adds insult to injury, placing additional stress on the people who have to deal directly with such employees.

WHAT PERPETUATES THE PERFORMANCE APPRAISAL MODEL?

Given all these difficulties in application, the resiliency of the traditional performance feedback model is impressive. Why has it persisted? One answer lies in the growing trend for dismissed employees to sue their former employers for wrongful dismissal. When such cases reach the courts, it is advantageous for an employer to be able to produce a performance evaluation scheme as evidence that performance has been managed responsibly. There it is in black and white: when and how often the performance deficiencies have been brought to the attention of the low performing employee, and what corrective action has been demanded.

It is a moot point as to how useful such a file actually is, since courts take a number of factors into consideration, such as age, length of service and expectations as to how long it will take dismissed employees to find comparable work. In spite of questions as to its relevance, employment lawyers continue to counsel the importance of a "file" documenting performance deficiencies, and human resource people have responded conscientiously by implementing or maintaining formal performance evaluation systems.

Another reason performance appraisal processes have continued to survive is that they address our most deeply felt values around fairness. They are based on the principle that people should be made aware of correctable actions which jeopardize their jobs. This is an admirable objective. Unfortunately, the message is rarely delivered intact or, when delivered, not heard.

And finally, the human resource professionals contribute to the model's survival because they tend to blame its problems on bad management rather than the complex dynamics of the model itself. Even when the effectiveness of a formal performance appraisal is mitigated by known factors, such as a strong union, the human resource department may still advocate performance appraisals, in the belief that they do some good for some people.

Despite all these problems, performance feedback is essential. It provides one of the crucial building blocks to development and it is absolutely essential to maintain fairness. The problem lies with the institutionalization of performance feedback. It can't be effectively systematized. It is imperative that people be provided with feedback that is relevant, trustworthy and ultimately, helpful. In short, performance feedback depends on an agreement: the person providing the feedback must care enough to confront constructively; and the person receiving feedback must accept that the feedback is given with the understanding that it is meant to be helpful rather than directive.

MULTI-SOURCE FEEDBACK

New methods of providing performance feedback have been developed, most notably "multi-source" feedback (also known as 360° feedback). In this model, several people who know a particular individual's work are asked to complete an evaluation form on a confidential basis. The form evaluates the extent to which the individual's behavior is perceived to be consistent with the organization's values and capabilities. The choice as to who completes the evaluation form is made by the person receiving the feedback and may include internal and external customers, as well as subordinates, colleagues and superiors (hence the term 360°). The feedback is summarized confidentially and the individual provided with a summarized report. Sometimes the feedback is delivered with the assistance of an external consultant or counselor who helps the individual understand how the information has been developed and how to extract the key messages from it.

The La Jolla, California-based firm of Keilty, Goldsmith and Boone (a.k.a. the KGB by friends of the firm) was one of the groups who pioneered the multi-source feedback concept. For the past 15 years or more, participants in its Excellent Manager Program have received multi-source feedback from people familiar with their leadership style. This feedback is integrated with classroom training on leadership concepts and best practices.

Multi-source feedback is receiving growing support and has become a widely-used technique whose major advantages are that it depersonalizes the feedback-giving process and reduces defensiveness on the part of feedback recipients. It is not, of course, without its limitations. My partner, George Toner, has considerable experience both in designing multi-source feedback processes and in counseling those receiving feedback. He has great confidence in the technique, but his experience has led him to question how much behavior actually changes as a result of feedback. He has encountered many situations in which people have rationalized critical feedback in a way that distorts or softens its substance. He and others are developing ways to improve the positive impact of multi-source feedback systems. For example, it helps to ask people to establish and review concrete action plans (although not the feedback), with their superiors or mentors. Evidence also suggests that the value of the system is enhanced by repetition, with its effectiveness increasing in the second, third and fourth year. Apparently, those providing the feedback tend to be more critical in later years if they have reason to believe that the individual has failed to respond to earlier feedback.

Ian Bruce is another Western Management Consultants colleague who is involved in multi-source feedback. His opinion is that, while the methodology does a fine job of identifying real problems, it is not as effective at bringing out concrete solutions. However, he sees that a number of trends will be helpful. Firstly, organizations are scheduling more frequent feedback and follow-up, as often as once every six months. This builds experience at setting concrete and measurable objectives to address the issues raised. While he agrees with George Toner that organizations may initially require people to share only their action plans with their boss and not the feedback itself, it is now more common to make sharing feedback mandatory. Not in year one, but every year thereafter. Individual feedback is to remain confidential between the person being assessed and his or her superior. However, it is very common for feedback of all participants to be aggregated and reported to senior management in consolidated form. Ian notes that the organizations he has worked with are encouraged by the fact that leadership ratings appear to be improving, suggesting that people are benefiting from the feedback.

Marshall Goldsmith, of Keilty, Goldsmith and Boone, investigated the effectiveness of providing feedback in a study that involved six major corporations with leaders from over 20 countries. The degree of change in perceived leadership effectiveness was closely related to the degree of follow-up. Managers who were seen as *not* following-up were perceived as only slightly more effective as a group than they were 18 months earlier. Managers who were perceived as having done some follow-up experienced a very positive shift in scores, with 89 percent rated as more effective. Goldsmith concludes that following-up the action plans their people develop results in a significant differentiating factor between effective and less effective managers.[2]

I was involved in one multi-source feedback process that tied the feedback scores to a variable income plan so that the better the feedback, the higher the bonus. The participants stated that the linkage between compensation and feedback made them reluctant to be critical, for fear that to do so would adversely affect their colleagues' compensation.

Despite these problems, multi-source feedback can be a useful tool, particularly where it's part of an integrated system of employee development and where it does not replace the responsibility of executives and managers to confront performance and behavior issues directly.

STRATEGIES TO CONFRONT BEHAVIOR AND PERFORMANCE EFFECTIVELY

Managers, starting with the CEO, need to ensure that performance and behavior problems are being addressed effectively—the guiding principle is to care enough to confront.

1. **Don't delay. Act on problem employees immediately.**

Behavior problems tend to be tougher than performance problems to address successfully. It's best to intervene earlier rather than later. The goal is to address behavior before it has become so deeply rooted it cannot be changed. Even though we may be tempted to avoid confrontation, this is one of the key tests of leadership.

2. **If the problem is one of attitude or behavior, position yourself as the coach in helping the person make the transition to more acceptable behavior.**

People who regard themselves as enjoying career success may be inclined to doubt that their own behavior is problematic. Often they will project ownership of the problem on to the leader expressing dissatisfaction. Means must be found to make the need for behavior change compelling enough that the individual will accept ownership for the problem and its solution. It is fairly common for organizations to seek assistance from a human resource executive or an external resource such as an industrial psychologist or coach.

---

[2] "The Leader of the Future: New Visions, Strategies and Practices for the Next Era," *Ask, Learn, Follow-Up and Grow*, Hesselbein, Goldsmith, Bekhard, Jossey-Boss.

Although this can be helpful, the leader must remain personally involved and demonstrate unwavering commitment to the need for change.

3. If the problem is one of substantive performance, be clear on the specific criteria the individual must meet as a condition of ongoing participation in his or her current role.

People have an amazing ability to rationalize critical feedback. It is uncanny how infrequently the person receiving negative feedback can accurately describe its essence. Consequently, we must strive to make the basis for rehabilitated performance crystal clear. This is usually more difficult than it sounds because of the rapidly changing circumstances in which most organizations operate and because measuring individual performance in today's team-based and process driven organizations is difficult. Nonetheless, failure to reach agreement on measurable criteria will probably make the problem worse, as both parties become more frustrated in their attempts to reconcile very different points of view.

4. Introduce some options within the performance management system.

Employees may resent the mandatory nature of many performance feedback systems, feeling that they are being controlled by a system without any voice in whether they wish to participate. It may be possible to design these systems in such a way that employees can opt to participate in some aspects and not others. For example, an integrated program could consist of:

- a performance contract specifying objectives and performance targets for a limited period
- a conventional performance appraisal, designed to assess the relative degree of success in achieving target performance
- a multi-source inventory and feedback process
- a skills and competency inventory
- an annual personal development plan
- a new performance contract for the next performance period

An individual's performance planning and development program could consist of a tailored mix of some or all of these six pieces. The enhanced effectiveness of such a program would be worth the more complicated administration.

Performance evaluation and feedback is an area in desperate need of innovation. Multi-source feedback is a promising direction but needs further development and refinement. The human dynamics involved are complex and highly individualistic. It is understandable for someone who is one year from retirement to choose the minimum level of involvement, but someone whose career is just beginning may want as much guidance as possible. It is unlikely that we can design a system which will serve everyone's needs well. Indeed, our attempts to do so have caused some of the difficulties. Formalized systems will never replace the need for good management. The need to confront unproductive attitudes and behaviors is a moral responsibility of leaders, not of systems.

5. Negotiate how negative feedback will be delivered.

No matter how effective an organization's performance management system, it still comes down to individual people communicating sensitive information to each other. I believe that people should negotiate with each other about how those who will be receiving the feedback prefer to receive it. Would they prefer a face-to-face meeting in an office, or a more informal setting such as an off-site coffee or meal-time meeting? Do they want suggestions as to how performance and behavior might be corrected, or do they just want the problem area clearly stated? Do they want ongoing feedback on how their attempts to address the issue are working, or do they want to be left alone? Would they prefer the information in writing, or verbally? Do they want anyone else, such as another manager or a personal friend, present at any discussion? (When language difficulties are involved, this can be a helpful measure for everyone.) Some families have adopted the practice of writing each other letters when confronting an emotionally hot issue. If feedback is delivered with sensitivity in a manner that respects the individual's preferences, it will do much to diffuse the emotional minefield. Anything that increases the comfort of both parties will be an improvement on the standard highly formalized appraisal interview, whose cold rigidity can be tough on both parties and highly destructive of relationships.

6. Try multi-source feedback.

Multi-source feedback is not only being more widely used, it is being used more effectively as organizations gain experience with it. There are many multi-source feedback products on the market, some of which are excellent. It is not difficult to design an in-house program—most organizations are capable of doing so. The feedback questionnaire needs careful crafting. It should reflect attitudes and behaviors which are important within the specific culture and also the kinds of values upon which the organization is trying to build future success. Some organizations that have designed their own multi-source feedback processes rely on outside consultants or advisors to meet with the feedback recipients to help them understand its implications and plan their response.

7. Review the organization's performance planning and evaluation processes.

Don't put too much faith in elaborate performance management systems. Leaders should set out to determine for themselves how effectively problem performers are managed. Certainly the leaders should make themselves aware of how valuable the performance management systems are perceived to be by both the managers who use them and employees who participate in them. How much trust do they have in the system? How accurately can people describe the specific performance outcomes for which they will be held responsible? Do the top leaders in the organization even use the official program? If not, why not?

In short, leaders should not assume that, just because a performance planning and evaluation process is in place, it is producing the desired results. Invest the effort required to review a few cases involving identified problem employees, in order to assess the effectiveness of the approach.

8. Provide collegial feedback.

Western Management Consultants treats feedback as part of our commitment towards each other as colleagues. Everyone in the firm, professionals or administrative staff, works together to develop two to three constructive suggestions for how each person could enhance his or her individual success. This is done thoughtfully and carefully and presented as advice which can be taken or not as each individual sees fit—in other words, as a gift.

9. Make sure that the system you use is completely aligned with the organization's culture.

At an accute care hospital, management set up a team of employees from all functions and all levels to develop a performance management system compatible with the hospital's new customer-centered, quality-oriented culture. They asked employees how they felt about the system and were astounded by the low level of understanding and trust in their program, which was based on the traditional model. They developed a new performance management process on a highly consultative basis, incorporating aspects of multi-source feedback on a voluntary basis, and training for all participants, regardless of whether they were conducting or participating in the performance appraisal. The resulting program achieved strong support throughout the entire organization. Interestingly, it was conceptually quite close to the traditional performance management model it replaced. The success of the new process can be attributed to the consultative approach in program design and also to the strong support the performance management process received from the hospital's leaders.

This is a good illustration of the fact that the technical elegance and design of the performance management system count less than the extent to which it is integrated and aligned with the organization's culture. Everyone observes with keen interest what leaders say and do in this area in particular, to assess how serious a matter performance and behavior really are. If they see the behavioral variances and problem performance consistently addressed as issues that leaders care about and act on, that will soon become the organizational norm.

Giving performance feedback effectively, in a manner that builds rather than destroys relationships, is no easy task. It requires better tools than have typically been available. And it requires more realism about the human dynamics involved. Part of the answer lies in refining the programs and experimenting with some of the more innovative feedback techniques, and part lies in caring enough to confront. Confrontation is a moral imperative. People must be able to trust that they will be told the truth about their performance and behavior.

CHAPTER **11**

MAKING ORGANIZATION CHANGE STICK

By now, it's rare for an organization not to have been involved in at least one major change process. I am certainly not the first to observe that most change processes—even those launched with the highest hopes—tend to flounder and lose energy, gradually fading until they pass quietly into the organization's history. For every organization that undergoes a change regarded as successful, there are perhaps dozens whose efforts have resulted in failure. Some change efforts even make the situation worse. And yet we plug on, implementing one change after another, hoping that the next will be the one that will work and fix everything so that the organization runs smoothly . . . until the next change. Are we expecting too much? What's the problem? Is it with the process or the objective or both? Why do we persist? Many change efforts remind me of a familiar definition of insanity: when we do the same things over and over again, hoping that the outcome will be different. If we want our change efforts to succeed, then we have to begin by changing the way in which we approach change in the first place.

We undertake change processes with the best of intentions: to improve effectiveness on a continuing basis by focusing everyone's commitment on the same set of goals. The most successful efforts involve statements of mission, vision and values, strong focus on customer satisfaction, emphasis on quality products and services and, above all, a desire to develop greater employee involvement, sense of ownership and sense of personal responsibility.

But the language used to announce organization change is often deceptive. It suggests that the primary goal is to change the *organization*. The reality is that the primary goal is almost always to change the way *people behave*. Change is frequently undertaken in response to a crisis or a succession of problems, such as poor financial performance, escalating costs, loss of valued staff, emergence of new competition or shareholder displeasure. Often, but not always, change initiatives are accompanied by organization downsizing and staff reduction, one of the reasons change initiatives may be somewhat suspect in the eyes of employees. Today, most organization change efforts are precipitated by CEOs who have decided that behavior such as rigidity, non-responsiveness or complacency can no longer be tolerated among the executive team, middle management, employees or perhaps all of them. They hope that the change will stimulate their people to develop new behavior and ways of working together that will enhance the organization. In short, it is *people*, not *organizations*, who must change.

ROADBLOCKS TO SUCCESS
UNREALISTIC EXPECTATIONS—THE RHETORIC OF CHANGE

The problem begins with our own expectations. When we talk about sustaining change we imagine a return to a stable, idyllic state after a period of change. Many of us subscribe to a widely accepted change model that encourages us to think of change as something that comes to an end. Kurt Lewin,[1] a well-known change guru, described change as a three-step process—unfreezing, changing and refreezing, a metaphor that has been sadly misunderstood. It's the "refreezing" that leads to problems. It implies a completion, a finish, a return to a "frozen" state. This is clearly unrealistic in contemporary organization life, and not at all what Lewin intended. He actually envisioned a continuous process of unfreezing, changing and refreezing where one set of changes are followed by another in a constant evolutionary pattern. Once we have unleashed the dynamics of change in an organization, can we really ever return to some idyllic static state?

The whole notion of "sustaining change" is a *non sequitur*. When we talk about sustaining change, we generally mean that we want a particular change-in-progress to become a permanent part of culture or operating style, not that we want the *state of change* to be sustained. But if we do in fact want the state of change to be an ongoing feature of organization existence, we will have to be clear on what we mean by "sustaining." Do we want to sustain the change or the *state* of change? Confusion over this distinction leads to severe practical difficulties. In practice, we often present organization change as a singular event from which we will move on. But the truth is that the climate of change

---

[1] *The Practical Theorist: The Life and Work of Kurt Lewin,* Teachers College Press, Teachers College, Columbia University, New York and London, 1977.

is here to stay. When we use rhetoric that suggests a return to a stable state, we do people a grave disservice. How can they make the preparations required to keep up and learn how to be a part of the future that demands continuous change? As difficult as it is, leaders have an obligation to accept change as a permanent feature of organization life. They help their colleagues most when they constantly challenge them to question their own assumptions and to organize their own aggressive, career-long learning strategies.

LEADERS WHO ARE UNPREPARED TO "WALK THE TALK"

It is difficult to imagine effective organization change taking place without the wholehearted commitment and active participation of senior leaders, particularly the CEO. I have encountered only one situation where apparently successful organization change was driven from below without the active support of the CEO. Creating internal commitment to a future vision is one of the fundamental expectations of leaders, as is their ability to ensure that the organization's plans, people and business processes are aligned with that vision.

Exceptions are almost always deadly. Why do executives imagine that everyone in the organization will understand when they make an exception to an agreement, or do something inconsistent with a stated value? Staff members of most organizations do not accept that principles and values apply to everyone except the leader, or that the principles apply sometimes but not always. People expect *more* from their executives, not less. Admittedly, leaders are in a difficult position, since they rarely receive reliable feedback about the impact of their actions on their credibility. People view violations of espoused values and principles seriously. Realistically, leaders may not be able to be completely consistent in all circumstances. It may be unreasonable for the rest of us to expect that of them. But reasonable or not, we are invariably disappointed when we suspect a significant gap between espoused values and actions. There is zero tolerance in this area.

The newly appointed chief operating officer of a not-for-profit organization I worked with made a grave error by failing to wait for the results of a number of task teams that were developing recommendations as part of a broader-based change process. He initiated actions and put his own program into place while encouraging the task teams to continue working. Team members suspected that his words of encouragement did not reflect the level of importance he really ascribed to what they were doing and the change process faded away.

We've all encountered similar experiences. My partner, Mary Baetz, worked with an organization whose president urged his management team to be innovative and risk taking in their approach to problem solving. But when one of the teams presented some ideas and recommendations to the president, his response was highly critical. He expressed disappointment that the team had not considered a number of issues he felt to be important. The team was surprised since they had not understood those issues to be within their mandate. When Mary subsequently explained how depressed the team was over his reaction and how it seemed inconsistent with the espoused values of innovation and risk taking, he was surprised and defensive.

LATE ADAPTERS

Can people change fast enough? Organization change consultants have long understood that employees adapt to change at different rates. Typically, the "missionaries" are in the forefront of the change process and highly identified with it. The "late adapters" may never be able to provide whole-hearted support. In the middle, we find the majority of people, the ones who experience initial reservations but ultimately decide to support an organized change process. Dealing with the late adapters is a matter of leadership and organization philosophy. Individual managers and staff members may be unaware that it is their behavior that is impeding change. They don't realize the effect they have on others who are more open-minded and want to participate in the process in a positive way. Some organizations feel that people who continue to resist and sabotage change should be told, in the words of one hospital CEO, to "catch the program or catch the bus." At the very least, such people do need feedback so that they know their behavior is seen as disruptive and unhelpful.

Claire Ross, the general secretary of a professional trade union, agrees that changing people's behavior may be too difficult to be practical within an organization, particularly when they have reservations about the direction of change. If the direction is clear to the senior management group, Ross recommends that it be implemented as quickly as possible. He seriously questions whether you can effectively combine the new and the old in a change process, and doubts that approaching a major change in small increments can ever be successful.

Although he believes that it is essential for people to be treated with respect and dignity, he acknowledges that it may be necessary to face up to the fact that some people will never participate constructively and need to leave the organization. When that is the case, Ross is emphatic that the organization should put its full resources behind helping these people find another assignment or to fairly reward their past contribution in some other creative way.

Peter Wolfraim is President of MFP Technology Services Ltd., a fast-growing lease financing and related management services company operating in the North American high technology finance market. Since its inception in 1984, the company has experienced continuous change in operations systems and organization, as it has fought to keep up with its own rapid expansion. For this company, perpetual change has been the reality. But even in such a young, dynamic high-tech company, people are struggling to keep up. Not only with the workload, but with the need to adapt to a larger, increasingly structured organizational environment.

Wolfraim has found it "unbelievably difficult to change people." Helping people understand and adapt to quickly changing roles and internal relationships has consumed much of his time. Although people agree at management meetings to support a course of action arrived at by consensus, they may not feel obligated to support the decision back in their departments. This well-known phenomenon of sandbagging (disclaiming responsibility for a group consensus of which you were a part) has impeded cross-department collaboration, something which MFP's business processes depend on heavily. The dysfunctionality of the executive team led a group of lower level managers to form their own operations group. It meets weekly and goes to the senior management team only when it has a recommendation requiring senior level support. Why? Because, as Wolfraim points out, the senior managers didn't make it happen. Reflecting on the experience, he wonders if people, particularly after they reach their 40s, are capable of very much change. He accepts that people, if forced, are capable of some modification in their behavior, but he wonders whether the investment of time and energy on the part of their organizational superiors may be too great to be practical.

Whether or not people are capable of fundamental change as individuals is a matter for social scientists. My experience mirrors that of Wolfraim's: as difficult as it can be, most people are capable of some behavior modification, particularly when it is a matter of personal survival. But the cost can be insupportable, not only in time and energy, but also in terms of the additional burdens that others must bear for the holdouts.

INADEQUATE SUPPORT FOR TEAMS

Much of the work of organization change is done in teams. In fact, teams are often the engine of change. Their success or failure tends to determine whether or not the overall change initiative will succeed. But few organizations are set up in a way to provide teams with the support they require to do their jobs well.

For example, organizations continue to reward people on the basis of individual performance plans negotiated with their own departmental superior. These plans often ignore or undervalue the work done in teams. And who is the person most likely to determine an individual's base compensation and any incentive compensation? The line superior, who is not in a position to have a good understanding of that individual's accomplishments as a member of a team.

Access to resources for teams is another problem area. Budgets, staff pools, access to technology and education all flow through the normal organizational channels, making it difficult for cross-functional teams to obtain required support. The demands of the team impose an extra work load on each of its members, who receive no corresponding relief from normal day-to-day duties. While members attend team meetings, work builds up back at the office, work that will have to be done on nights or weekends. No wonder we're seeing a growing resistance to being appointed as part of a change or process improvement team.

Leaders face a great challenge in remaining open-minded about the information and the recommendation provided by the teams working on a change effort. The assessments and recommendations of such teams can be flawed and biased. Some recommendations may be quite disappointing, especially if they focus on relatively unimportant aspects of a situation. But senior executives can give the teams working in the interest of constructive change a very rough ride, sometimes more than they deserve. Senior people must work in partnership with those to whom they have delegated significant change responsibility, by being open to information they may not immediately accept, and by working with teams to improve the quality and practicality of their recommendations.

INTERNAL POLITICS

All organizations have politics. Bad relations between departments promote politics. Strong opposing opinions of key executives or managers promote politics. Any jockeying for a favorable position in the competition for promotion is a virtual breeding ground for politics. Even strong personal likes or dislikes among influential individuals can lead to politics. And politics can torpedo a change effort. As soon as politics become involved, people begin to suspect that support for the official position is less than solid.

The political dimension of change may be overt and intentional, as in the case when people withhold support for key change initiatives sponsored by rivals, in order to prevent the initiative and the rival from succeeding. Or the politics may operate on a more subtle, even unintentional level. This is often the case when teams engage in vigorous debate of ideas and proposals but expect all team members to support decisions reached by consensus. Even highly principled and well-intentioned people find this expectation difficult to live with.

The following experience, typical of many organizations, illustrates how a host of significant problems, political and otherwise, can be raised when making decisions by consensus. The chairperson of a sub-committee objected to a decision of the standing committee to which the sub-committee reported. In consideration of her concerns, a special meeting was convened. It included all members of the standing committee, several members of senior staff and an external consultant who was being paid for his time. Several participants attended during normal working hours, at considerable inconvenience. The group worked through the objections of the sub-committee chairperson point by point, in an effort to find compromises without destroying the integrity of the project. At the end of the half-day meeting, they had worked out a number of compromises, but the sub-committee chairperson was still unhappy. It was difficult for the other ten participants to see where further compromise could be made, but all were concerned that the sub-committee chairperson would report back negatively to her sub-committee. All present realized this could lead to further dissatisfaction and further proliferation of the original concerns. What to do? This was an issue of pure politics, since the sub-committee chairperson was the only person who felt that substantive issues remained. In fact, further compromise would have been counterproductive. The situation, which strained everyone's patience, demonstrates the under-lying limitations of a decision by consensus philosophy under conditions where minority views cannot be resolved.

Collaboration and cooperation between organization units, and the elimi-nation of destructive politics are among the most frequently desired change objectives. Ironically, the change process itself can be the source of political activity. Consequently, change processes are often co-opted by the very people to whom they are directed. This is why Claire Ross, with his considerable experience with school boards, believes that an organization change strategy should be radical and that it should be implemented quickly. If change is introduced incrementally, he observes, those opposed to the change will use the existing organizational paradigm against it.

Interfunctional conflict and rivalry may be difficult to overcome, especially when the competing groups are separated physically or when there is competition for resources such as budget or access to information technology.

However, politics cannot be completely avoided. Political differences between corporate and divisional offices seem inescapable, especially when offices are located in different regions of the country. Change leaders understand that there is usually an important political dimension to a change initiative that cannot safely be ignored or discounted.

PAYING LIP SERVICE TO CHANGE

Virtually every organization has a mission, vision and values. If we were to assemble the statements of mission, vision and values of several organizations and blank out the name of the organizations, it would be difficult to tell them apart. It seems to me that most mission statements are built around the same three themes: quality customer service, excellent staff and good products and services. Is this because these are enduring truths or is does it simply reflect a lack of imagination?

It's difficult to avoid becoming inured to these words and concepts. They are losing their power to stir us. People are tired of the language of contemporary change management. This is a significant problem. For a collective groan, consider "empowerment." Certainly it is right up there at the top of the list of phrases that people love to hate. Yet empowerment describes one of the most important improvement opportunities available to many organizations. There are those who will argue that "empowerment" is just a fancy word for "delegation." But the concept of delegation is slightly different, suggesting something more temporary and limited. The leader must find fresh and interesting ways to articulate a clear direction for the organization, to avoid sounding platitudinous.

Even the most elegantly expressed statements of mission, vision and value will lose relevance in the light of new external circumstances. But if they have to be redefined frequently, the problem rests with how well they have been defined in the first place. The temptation is to redefine and rewrite these fundamental expressions of corporate direction without reflecting adequately on how relevant they continue to be. Often, the leaders are the first to become bored with significant planning or organization change initiatives. This arouses cynicism about future "flavor of the month" initiatives which people will tend to discount as nothing more than the latest enthusiasm of the boss.

Admittedly, things can change with breathtaking speed in organizations. New issues arise, new crises strike, and the executive team has to stay on top of them all. Taking the time to link everything back to the change process may not seem practical in the heat of the moment. The new crisis requires immediate response. People are expected to drop everything to help out. Team meetings, process reviews, and all-staff meetings are pushed back on the agenda for the most understandable of reasons, but at a very high cost to their continued relevance and importance. The only solution is to build contingency plans into the change process, in order to make sure it stays on track no matter what emergencies arise.

HOW TO SUSTAIN REAL ORGANIZATION CHANGE

1. Require leaders to model the new behavior.

In the area of organizational leadership, actions speak louder than words. People will watch what leaders actually do and value, in order to determine how serious the change process really is. For example, many organizations articulate career-long learning as a value but do not make time or financial support available to those who have asked for it. Similarly, if the change is designed to empower people to make decisions which they have the information and opportunity to make, leaders cannot interfere, second guess, or express displeasure when that initiative is exercised.

Fortunately, there are also many examples of effective modeling. Bill Etherington of IBM visibly followed his company's new business casual dress code, thereby demonstrating that it was acceptable to shed suits and ties in situations defined by the guidelines. Claire Ross took responsibility for one of the issues teams formed as part of his union's new management style and subjected himself to the attendant peer review process in the same way as everyone else.

Perhaps the leader's greatest role in sustaining organization change is to remain steadfast. Keep it high on the executive committee agenda, continue to ask for progress reports, ensure that the necessary resources are provided. Continue to ask about it, encourage people who are working on it, and demonstrate key values. These are all ways that it can be sustained. The leader can't allow the change process to die, or the next initiative will have no chance whatsoever. An unsuccessful change process is a defeat and, in undeniable part, a personal defeat for a CEO.

As discussed earlier, core processes may need to be modified in order to support teamwork. If individuals spend significant time involved in teamwork, this must be reflected in their performance objectives and contracts, performance evaluation and reward systems.

Team leaders need access to resources; so the means by which they can gain access must be in place. Some project management-based organizations have set up key support groups to facilitate the work of the project teams These groups address needs such as budget and financial management, information technology and project team staffing.

2. Plan change with lots of input.

Since organization change requires a change in people's behavior, it is a good idea to consult with the people involved, in order to develop a strategy for change. Some organizations consult with customers or staff or both. When the finance function of an electric utility wanted to introduce an improvement initiative, they first canvassed staff in order to learn which issues and opportunities for improvement the staff saw as important. Next, they conducted external research to identify the available models. After considering business process reengineering and quality customer service, they chose a continuous improvement model as best meeting needs identified through their internal consultation. Because they could demonstrate how the developing program mirrored staff input, they were on very solid ground.

External change consultants can play a useful role in evaluating an organization's existing environment and recommending a tailored approach to organization change. Generally, tailored approaches are more successful than "off the shelf" approaches. With the latter, there's always the risk that someone will become enamored of a particular system or model and successfully recommend its implementation. This assumes that a strategy that has worked elsewhere will work anywhere. These packaged approaches tend to have more than their fair share of jargon. They also may require highly structured tools and methods which are at risk of rejection when transplanted in your organization.

Prospects of developing a successful organization change intervention increase when the initiative is based on clear understanding of the needs of the organization. Such an understanding can be gained only by asking soft questions (regarding perceptions, values and attitudes) in addition to the harder questions (regarding systems, processes and operations). People are aware of the issues and impediments that stand in the way of improved effectiveness and will, given half a chance, communicate them. At the same time, they may not be aware of all of the factors and challenges upon which future success will depend. And for that reason I usually recommend a mixed group of inside and outside people to conduct the review and develop the recommended plan.

3. Acknowledge limits.

The brutally high expectations of leaders on the part of employees and the general public have made it virtually impossible for leaders to acknowledge that they may not know what to do or, alternatively, have done the wrong thing in a given set of circumstances. But for a leader to acknowledge the difficulties which everyone knows exist may not harm the credibility of the change process at all. It may, in fact, enhance it.

Gwenlyn Setterfield, executive director of an organization that funds arts programs, was strongly challenged by her management team because a new organization change was having some negative as well as positive effects on their roles and job satisfaction. Gwenlyn's approach was to acknowledge the validity of the complaints while admitting that she was not entirely certain of how to deal with those impacts, nor did she feel she was solely responsible for managing them. This led to a constructive discussion and ultimately, a plan to manage the impacts of change.

4. Construct a framework of real team support.

Teams can perform a valuable role in organization change. In fact, it's difficult to imagine how successful change can be achieved without teams. They consult widely, consider options and develop recommendations for constructive change, which are typically presented to a steering committee or an executive group. They can provide an effective means of breaking down departmental barriers. They can establish significant independence from the cultures and political agendas of the normal organization structure. By their very nature they are flexible—they may have relatively short life spans, or they may be ongoing, depending on the nature of the change effort.

Many people, especially those most highly regarded by the organization, are spending more of their time working in a team setting. People who have been part of successful teams may reap considerable benefits in terms of prestige and career prospects, but the fundamental human resources policies of most organizations have not kept pace. Many organizations still need to develop a framework of real team support. Such a framework should include the following three key elements:

- access to resources for teams such as staff, technology, information and budget
- ways to recognize and reward a person's team contribution

- integration of the teams with the organization's structure

Each team must have its own integral place in the organization's structure and be treated accordingly. Their absence on the official organization chart is a strong indicator that they are not adequately connected to other basic processes. People management systems need to be less position bound than has been the case traditionally, in order to reflect the reality of what is actually going on and to ensure that people will continue to be willing to contribute to special initiatives.

5. **Integrate the values and objectives of change with the core business processes of the organization.**

Mixed messages have a tendency to cancel each other out, resulting in aborted change efforts. Begin by examining those processes which most affect people, such as planning, budgeting, staff selection, compensation and communications, to ensure that they are absolutely consistent with the new direction and values. For example, compensation plans that have a variable income component based on individual performance may be incompatible with a culture emphasizing teamwork and collaboration. Similarly, top-down planning processes may not fit with cultures in which staff members are expected to exercise their judgment regarding how to satisfy challenging customer demands. These examples may seem obvious, but it is astounding how often we find that the values and objectives of change are inconsistent with the core business processes of the organization.

EVALUATE EMPLOYEE REACTION DURING THE CHANGE PROCESS

Since changing people's behavior is one of the fundamental objects of organization change initiatives, it makes sense to regularly evaluate how effective employees perceive the initiatives to be.

However, external consultants who conduct assessments by survey or by interview often meet with resistance. This is understandable for three reasons:

- Because it takes time for the change process to gain momentum, leaders know that employees will not have experienced much change;
- Executives may feel that they are in touch with employee attitudes and don't need a survey;
- People are "surveyed to death."

Nevertheless, it is a good idea to ask employees for their opinions about whether the change strategy is proving helpful. If an employee survey has been conducted prior to the development of the change process, a simple approach is to repeat it after six or twelve months to measure the degree of change. Their feedback can uncover good ideas and be energizing, at a time when enthusiasm for the change effort is lagging. Problem areas which may have turned up in the pre-change period often prove to be surprisingly persistent.

Employee perceptions of managed change programs can be surprisingly negative, especially if employee cynicism is increasing in general, for reasons discussed in Chapter 5. But even if employees are not cynical, they may think that the responsibility to address problems belongs to senior management alone. In any case, it is natural for people to resist change. And this can lead to distrust and misunderstandings of intentions and actions. The failure to take stock from time to time can jeopardize the enormous investment organizations have made.

6. Deal with the late adapters.

Everyone deserves time and support to adapt to changes that may involve principles which they truly cannot accept. Change consultants advise that an organization can expect somewhere between 5 percent and 20 percent of the workforce to be holdouts—people who will never accept the need for change or the validity of the initiatives being implemented in order to achieve it. Many of the late adapters will have a destructive effect by ridiculing, criticizing, demonizing leaders, withholding information and preventing people who report to them from participating. There are countless ways of resisting change. But ultimately, resistance must cease. Very senior people in the organization usually have no difficulty tolerating the cynics and critics; their effect is most destructive for those who work in close contact with them, especially people organizationally junior to them. Leaders owe it to the little people in the organization to deal with the more intractable forms of resistance. In the final analysis, everyone needs to move on.

Ending does not necessarily require firing. That should occur as only a last resort. First, the late adapters should be given direct feedback about the fact that their behavior is destructive. Some people will be surprised to learn that they are perceived as problems, and will adjust their behavior accordingly. Others will argue that their actions are justifiable because of their conviction that the change initiative is misguided. Obviously, in a democracy people are entitled to their beliefs but not to harm others. These people need to be asked whether they will be able to modify the destructive aspect of their behavior. Hopefully, they will be able to accommodate themselves to the need to support organizational direction. In the event they are unable to do so, there should be a candid discussion as to what is to be done. Ultimately, if a person cannot provide some constructive support to the organization's direction, they should, as a matter of principle, be prepared to go to another organization whose objectives they can support.

CHAPTER 12

COMMUNICATING THE TRUTH, THE WHOLE TRUTH, AND NOTHING BUT THE TRUTH

"There are lies and there are lies."
—U.S. Democratic Party representative commenting on
President Clinton's denials of sexual wrong-doings

I wish I had a dollar for every time I've heard someone in an organization say, "This is a communication problem," or "We have to improve communication around here." It's a pretty safe bet that in discussions of any complex problem someone will attribute the problem to poor communication. In fact, the term "communication" is so overused that it has become almost meaningless.

What do people mean when they complain about communication? Very often they believe that they are failing to receive the information they need in order to do their jobs well. In this case, the problem is a lack of communication. People can be left in the dark because organizations simply don't have the time for adequate communication of information.

But often when people complain, they are referring not to the amount of information received, but to the credibility of that information. This is an increasingly voiced complaint that goes right to the heart of the how people feel about their organization and their leaders. The *Concise Oxford English Dictionary* defines communication as the act of imparting information, and also as a connection between places, such as a common door or passageway. This secondary meaning relates to the challenge of organizational communication. If the leader's communication fails to connect to people's understanding of what is real and important, or worse, is perceived as merely gilding the lily, then credibility and trust are eroded. I have frequently heard leaders express dismay over the enormous damage following relatively small slips and

145

lapses in communication. What they don't seem to realize is that the nature of trust is cumulative—it is built up over time. It can also be destroyed in an instant. Or, like that small spot of rust on your car, if it isn't attended to, it will eat away at the metal and destroy it.

CERTAIN TRUST-BUSTERS

Over the past decade or so, organizations have adopted several common practices that severely undermine people's trust and acceptance. The propensity to give every message an exclusively positive spin, regardless of the fact that an issue may have seriously negative features, is particularly damaging, as is the use of jargon and euphemisms to obfuscate the true meaning of sensitive issues. Both of these practices distort meaning and create distance between sender and receiver. When that distance becomes too great, the connection breaks, with an inevitable increase in mutual distrust.

1. **The age of positive spin.**

Somewhere along the way it became *de rigueur* to emphasize only the positive aspects of decisions, actions or events. Public relations professionals are often called upon to put a positive spin on the fall-out of corporate mergers. Typically, announcements of such mergers will focus on enthusiastic descriptions of the potential new business opportunities, with very little said about potential job loss. The initial announcement of the proposed merger of two major banks, for example, glossed over several important concerns. These were addressed only in response to strong adverse response by the media and the public. Then was it acknowledged that some branches might be closed, with the attendant job loss. But the information, when it came, seemed grudging and defensive, almost as if the banks had been trying to hide something. Critics of the banking industry had a field day.

On a less dramatic level, we have only to think of how the communication of something like a new internal computer system almost always emphasizes the benefits of the system without mentioning the impact on workload, the probable glitches and other aspects of these changes which people know they are likely to encounter.

It is difficult to understand how we arrived at the point where leaders believe they must speak in glowing terms about situations which clearly have down-sides as well as up-sides. I suspect that we have the late Dr. Spock to thank, at least in part, for our faith in positive spin. He almost single-handedly influenced an entire generation to believe in the importance of a positive self-image. The idea that critical feedback should be avoided lest it do damage to the tender psyche of our youth is pervasive in our society. Many baby boomers raised under this philosophy seem to hear any criticism as negative and destructive. The concern is that negative news will demoralize people. Negative reinforcement is thought to undermine self-concept and self-confidence, leading to anxiety and fear. If people are anxious, the argument goes, it is difficult to sustain positive energy and a willingness to take reasonable risks. Leaders feel it is better to build on the positives in the situation and to de-emphasize negative implications which, after all, may or may not develop. Wouldn't it be wonderful if life were that simple and we really could eliminate the bad by praising the good!

The work of the eminent behaviorist, B. F. Skinner, has also had a huge impact on our attitude towards criticism. Skinner set out the theoretical basis for the generally accepted notion that positively reinforcing desired behavior is more effective than punishing the undesirable.

INSTITUTIONALIZATION OF POLLYANNA

Belief in power of positive thinking is so profound that we have institutionalized it in countless ways. We have even created a whole new profession of "spin doctors" whose job is to manage and massage the communication to present the message (and those who deliver it) in the most positive light. We do not think twice about putting the best face on things, we just do it. This was taken to a satirical extreme in *Wag the Dog*, a movie in which Dustin Hoffman played a Hollywood producer hired by a presidential spin doctor. His assignment was to create an entirely fictitious war with Albania in order to take the heat off the President of the United States, who had been implicated in a sexual encounter with a minor. The goal was to position the President as a national hero so that he could regain the population's respect before the upcoming election.

The ancient Greek warriors knew that the bearer of bad news must be cautious, an experience many of us have seen mirrored in our own organizational lives. Peter Wolfraim is the founder and President of MFP, a high-growth company operating in the technology leasing field. He relates a story of a manager who was part of an organization-wide communication program to explain some impending changes in work processes. Because the changes had the potential of leading to job loss, the communication plan was very carefully crafted by the senior management team. The managers agreed that they would emphasize the positive features of the changes while acknowledging that there was the potential for some downsizing. Peter was determined that the message would be consistently delivered across the organization and asked his human resources director to sit in on the meetings to ensure that was the case. In one meeting, the manager made the presentation and was asked by a staff member about the effects of what he had to say on job security. Unbelievably, he replied that there would be no negative impact on his department, none whatsoever. How can such truth-bending communication be explained? The answer can only lie in the extent to which we are conditioned to believe in communicating in exclusively positive terms, even when doing so leads to serious distortions of the truth.

This is a time in organizational life when people are feeling so anxious about matters of employment security that they crave straight talk even if that involves hearing bad news.

CONFLICT AVOIDANCE

Part of this tendency may be nothing more than a wish to avoid dealing with an unpleasant situation. Our wish is to avoid all the problems that arise when we speak of the negative implications or outcomes of a situation or decision. But we're sticking our heads in the sand if we think that by not admitting the downside, we won't have to deal with it. Acknowledging the negative may be more problematic in the short term, but not to do so is more problematic in the long term. (Just look at what happened to President Clinton.)

People actually receive training from public relations consultants on the techniques of answering the question they *wish* had been asked, instead of the question that was really asked. Originally developed to meet the needs of politicians, such training has been provided by some companies to their executives as a means of helping them deal with the media or with difficult public appearances. The problem is that the technique has been overused to such an extent that it is frequently as transparent as the finest crystal, and just as easily shattered. In 1999, a provincial political leader was interviewed on a news radio program about an ugly public sector strike. The topic was how he would have handled the situation. The only point that was clear about that interview was his steadfast commitment to evading all of the tough questions that were put to him and instead, responding to questions that *hadn't* been asked. But he didn't fool the listeners for one minute. As soon as the interview was over their angry phone calls started coming in, and many of them were aired.

HOW MUCH DO PEOPLE NEED TO KNOW?

Problems invariably arise when people base their communication decisions on vague principles and shallow assumptions. Management teams, for example, frequently find themselves in discussion about what should and should not be communicated to customers and employees. They may be wary of open communication, which is certainly understandable. If they acknowledge errors, they may face questions of legal liability. If they share highly detailed financial, compensation or benefits information, they may be concerned about misinterpretation of that information by unions representing their employees. Communication directed at employee groups must catch the right balance between enough and too much detail and it is all too easy to get this balance wrong.

I am a member of a not-for-profit board which had to decide how much financial information to provide to members prior to their completing a survey relating to the future of certain programs. Views varied widely from those who felt members should be provided with a full report comprising some 28 pages of data, to those who felt members should complete the questionnaire without benefit of any background information. What I found most interesting were the widely different assumptions that individual board members made about communication. The differences were partly ideological, with some people convinced that members are entitled to know everything and others equally convinced that elected leaders have a mandate to make decisions in accordance with their individual judgment as directors. Anyone with experience in organizations will recognize this situation.

When making decisions about how much people should know, the challenge is to do so for the right reasons. In this particular situation, for example, it was reasonable to assume that not everyone would want to wade through 28 pages of dense numerical data. Instead, people could have been provided with a summary of the financial information and an invitation to call the organization's financial staff if they wanted more details. That would have been a sensible approach and one that was respectful of members.

To withhold information on the basis that only the board members have a right to the information or know enough to interpret it properly, is belittling and insulting. I am always uncomfortable when I hear people make sweeping generalizations about what those who are not present ought and ought not to know about issues. When the assumptions appear to be grounded in a kind of elitism, an attitude that only the leaders have the experience and judgment to reach intelligent conclusions, it's time to worry.

Organization veterans have been in this situation many times. They have attended countless meetings in which agreements have been reached as to what will and will not be communicated to people who are not present at the meeting. The problem is that there is such a fine line between deciding not to communicate a certain aspect of the situation and not telling the truth. My experience has been that most leaders and managers are conscientious, principled people who are reluctant to consciously tell a lie but who nevertheless are reasonably comfortable with a high degree of management of the message of communication. Unfortunately, this tendency can easily be misunderstood as something devious, and there is a high cost in leadership credibility and certainly a lack of buy-in to decisions which are described in ways that arouse suspicion.

Leaders are often faced with a Hobson's choice, since the cost of communicating the truth in the form of unpopular decisions can be so high. A vicious circle can occur when leaders who communicate candidly are then punished for delivering bad news, thereby making them reluctant to be as candid in the future. Still, there is no real option to straight and honest communication. Its absence will have consequences if not now, then when it becomes apparent in the future. As the saying goes, "the truth will out."

2. Jargon and euphemisms.

The use of euphemisms and jargon can undermine the credibility of communication. Matthew Ingram, in his review of Andrew S. Grove's book *Only the Paranoid Survive*, comments on the destructive effects of business jargon: " . . . a management book isn't seen as worthy unless it is filled with shifting paradigms, achievement plateaus and acronyms . . ."[1] Communication today is filled with euphemisms which fool nobody in their attempts to use nice language to mask unpleasant truths. Not long ago, I participated in an exercise at a management workshop where the task was to see how many commonly used euphemisms we could come up with that meant, in essence, to fire someone. Within minutes we had come up with 10, and I know there are many more. People can be made redundant, downsized, right sized, impacted by restructuring, dehired, freed up, transitioned, outplaced, laid off, or outsourced. But never *fired*.

The proclivity of organizational people to use jargon provides a wellspring of humor. Matthew Ingram had great fun with strategic inflection points (SIP), a fine example of how astoundingly awkward jargon can be. Based on

---

[1] *Globe & Mail*, Saturday, November 2, 1996. Review by Matthew Ingram of *Only the Paranoid Survive*, Andrew S. Grove, Doubleday.

my personal survey, the two most hated words in the business lexicon are "empowerment" and "paradigm." But "reengineering" is closing the gap, which is probably a reflection of the fact that people suspect it is used to cloak actions such as downsizing and lay offs.

The resistance to jargon has grown so intense that some people take exception even to some perfectly innocent words. I was startled to hear that a participant at a workshop I was facilitating considered "values" a buzzword, and I'm still wondering what I would do if I could not use it freely. On another occasion, I was working on a planning initiative with the senior staff and volunteers of a nation-wide professional association. The Executive Director groaned out load when a board member suggested that what we needed was a team vision to guide us through our workshop. The ED said "if you use words like 'vision' people's eyes will glaze over."

We may think that the use of jargon demonstrates that we're in touch with the latest thinking, that we understand the concepts being used in organizations today. And to some extent that's true. But at the same time, it's a good thing to bear in mind that the knowledge expressed through the use of jargon is generally only skin deep. When people have a deeper knowledge of a subject, they generally express it in plain English. Einstein's theory of relativity is so lucidly (and elegantly) written, for example, that you don't need to be a physicist to understand it.

Jargon can also be very damaging. In some organizations, the importance of providing equal opportunity for under-represented groups may be impeded by discomfort with language; the search to find inoffensive terms to refer to the people involved. Unfortunately, when we go to extremes to avoid giving offense our efforts can have the opposite effect. The more delicate our terms, the more likely that they will be heard as contemptuous or distrustful of the people to whom we are referring. In reality, such terms merely reflect our fear that we will be committing a *faux pas*. The language which has resulted, if not downright insulting, is awkward at best, rolling off the tongue like a mouthful of grit.

The use of jargon and euphemisms makes more complex the already tricky business of communicating clearly. The more the buzzwords are used, the more they lose meaning. Rather than appearing knowledgeable, people who rely on them appear slick, shallow and untrustworthy. No wonder we lose patience with them.

Similarly, the tendency to put a positive spin on all messages, no matter how negative, erodes our trust in the truth and the honesty of the communicator. In 1996 there was a media frenzy about whether golf superstar Tiger Woods was going to turn pro. Although he must have completed negotiations with sponsor Nike at the time, Woods seemed to treat the matter as an unfounded rumor. Was that because media pressure can make it impossible to tell the truth? Or was it because the media somehow does not deserve the truth?

STRATEGIES TO COMMUNICATE CREDIBILITY

Every time any piece of information is communicated within an organization, an opportunity arises to communicate the organization's credibility or lack of credibility. Since communication errors are very damaging, it is worthwhile to work hard at getting it right.

1. Involve leaders in face-to-face communication.

One of the participants in a Western Management Consultants' recent research project in organization change stated that the *principal* role of the modern leader is to communicate with all stakeholders, including employees. Although leadership involves more than communication, people do look to the leader as the source of information and assurance about what is going on. Even in very large organizations, face-to-face or at least voice-to-voice communication can be a reality. One CEO we work with communicated simultaneously with employees throughout the many locations of the company through an electronic hookup that broadcast employees' questions and his replies through the public address system.

2. Make straight talk the expectation.

In 1994, Western Management Consultants conducted focus group discussions with senior managers of over 100 companies regarding their experiences with organization change. We learned that the need for "straight talk" was one of the key issues.[2]

Employees are reaching the end of their tolerance for unclear, ambiguous and deliberately managed communication. There is a need for change. Communication is one of the key ways in which organizations create and manage expectations. The theme should be straight talk. Organizations need to become more comfortable with communicating in a straightforward fashion and acknowledging the parts of a situation which are either unclear or undecided.

Being realistic is preferable to creating expectations that will be hard to live up to. Every organization has its pessimists and optimists and messages should be designed to fit into the middle ground. Pointing out the good and

---

[2] "Organization Change," *Western Management Newsletter*, September 1993.

the bad will be welcome. Things rarely unfold in exactly the way intended and we generally respect people who tell us both sides of the story. Leaders and managers need to become more comfortable with being strongly challenged, sometimes in a way that seems hostile, as employees take advantage of the opportunity to put "the suits" on the hot-seat. A simpler, more balanced style of communication will ultimately achieve greater credibility than the spun-sugar style of the past. Communication specialists can be helpful in advising and supporting this simpler, straighter form of communication.

3. Avoid buzzwords and euphemisms.

As in the case of excessively managed messages, tolerance for jargon and indirect language is rapidly declining. If jargon is necessary, then the meaning of the terms should be explained clearly. If it is necessary to use some of the most hated words, such as "empowerment," "paradigm," and "business process reengineering," they should be used sparingly.

4. Tell the truth, and insist that others do as well.

Leaders rarely tell overt untruths; their errors are more likely to be:

- untruths of omission, as in the case of not mentioning expected job loss in connection with a reorganization
- untruths of exaggeration, where the positive benefits may be overstated
- untruths of expectation, where people are encouraged to believe in an uncertain outcome

Leaders need to become more demanding of themselves about the messages they communicate and they must apply the same standards to their colleagues. Transparent leadership is impossible without transparent communication.

5. Acknowledge difficulties and areas in which the answer is not yet clear.

This advice is very challenging because it will not come naturally to a generation of leaders trained to seem always in command and fully knowledgeable. But a candid admission that they don't have all the answers makes them seem more human and avoids the kind of glibness which makes employees uncomfortable. Most importantly, significant facts and information about problem areas should not be withheld from the people they affect. It outrages people to find out after the fact something that they could have been told earlier.

6. Find workable methods for two-way communication.

Organizations have always tried to create a climate of dynamic two-way communication, generally with mixed success. Fads come and go—suggestion boxes, CEO hot-seat meetings, employee advisory committees, bulletin boards (electronic or otherwise), telephone hotlines, and so on. Most have a relatively short life span.

Many senior managers have expressed their frustration with an ongoing paradox involving employees who demand more communication but who seem less willing than ever to participate personally in it. Notwithstanding the difficulties, a real effort needs to be made to encourage a climate in which employees actively participate in a two-way communication process. Expectations that they do so should be made very clear and sustained over time. Encouraging people to participate even when they are very busy is important if two-way communication is to become part of the fundamental operating style of the organization.

7. Try the technology.

Information technology has revolutionized communication, but there are great differences in how effectively organizations use this new technology. The most promising tools are e-mail, voice mail, electronic bulletin boards, cellular phones and conferencing by telephone or video.

While cost must be taken into consideration when determining which technology to use, resistance to it should not be a factor. Serious questions have been raised as to how the communication technology affects our personal and working lives, but it is fruitless to resist its introduction. Failing to make use of available technology simply causes people to be left behind in the quest for increasing productivity. In any case, people who have learned to use technology-driven communication tools quickly wonder how they could have managed without them. It wasn't very long ago when people positively *hated* voice-mail. Today, most of us can appreciate its convenience.

We've known for a long time that the retention of written information is alarmingly low. As the pace of working life quickens, face-to-face meetings are not always practical. Technology may not be a perfect answer, but it *is* an answer. It is not really a question of whether the new communication tools will be used, it's a question of when and how well.

It is difficult to separate leadership and communication in today's organizations. The credibility of the communication is integral to the credibility of the leadership. The significance of small errors in communicating have a tendency to be magnified. Organizations need to hold themselves to very high standards in this area.

Fortunately, we have some positive models of credible communication. The way in which Tylenol handled the poisoning of their product is now considered the textbook on communicating honestly, respectfully and transparently under pressure. Jean Charest gained respect for openly sharing the process by which he decided to take on the leadership of the Quebec Liberals, a decision he clearly found agonizing to make. Ontario Hydro's recent struggles illustrate both the bad and the good. The Hydro Corporation was seriously damaged by news that it had, for some time, failed to divulge radioactive emissions into Lake Ontario. However, Chairman Bill Farlinger set a more positive tone in the courageous way he acknowledged Hydro's nuclear difficulties and specified the steps Hydro was planning to take to overcome them. These examples all show how telling the good together with the bad in plain language is not only possible, it can be done in a manner that builds leadership credibility.

CHAPTER **13**

SHOW ME THE MONEY

The subject of employee compensation has long been considered fair game by the media. They have always paid attention to union disputes and settlements. Media coverage has also reflected a growing interest in compensation as an integral part of the battle for gender equality. Wage differentials between men and women have helped bring the subject of compensation into the public domain. But not until 1991, when some whopping CEO pay packages were disclosed in the media, did the subject of executive compensation fully emerge into the spotlight. No longer a nice, quiet backwater of organization life, it causes considerable embarrassment and contributes to the mood of cynicism sweeping corporate North America.

When new legislation in Ontario required public disclosure of public-sector and near-public-sector cash compensation over $100,000 per annum, the media responded with enthusiasm. "CEO's Paid Double That of Senior Executives, Study Shows," read one disapproving headline of a 1996 newspaper article detailing a Sobeco Ernst & Young survey of TSE 300 companies. And that was typical of hundreds of such headlines in newspapers across Canada. Public outcry to the disclosures was swift. Reactions ranged from surprise to outrage.

PERCEPTION IS EVERYTHING

Fortune magazine has been tracking the issue of executive compensation since 1991 when it published "How Much CEO's Really Make," by Graef Crystal, a well known critic of executive compensation practices. His displeasure in the "great CEO pay bash" is abundantly clear.[1] "Excesses of this past year produced an outcry that has finally been heard in boardrooms," he writes.

---

[1] "How Much CEO's Really Make," by Graef Crystal, *Fortune Magazine*, June 1991.

"Outside directors in particular are confiding to friends that they have gotten the message. Next year will be different, they say. If that's true, the change won't come a moment too soon. The pay issue has brought top managers of many big companies to the brink of losing all credibility with their employees and society at large."

Crystal describes as a "real whopper" the $39 million compensation received by Time Warner's CEO Steven Ross. Ross could argue that this figure includes the value of stock options in the year when they were exercised. A similar problem arises with much of the survey information on CEO compensation because the relation between CEO compensation and performance is not always clear and can sometimes seem arbitrary.

Sibson & Company, a respected human resource and compensation consulting firm, tackled the growing executive pay controversy in an article entitled "Unimpeachable Executive Pay."[2] Sibson fully expects the media to continue to harangue corporate America regarding executive pay levels. While the article maintains that "greedy CEO's and easily swayed executive compensation committees are the exception, not the norm," it also maintains that "most CEO's and boards want executive pay programs that align executive pay with returns to shareholders." Absolutely. The problem has less to do with greed than with compensation plan design and administration of compensation plans. But the public perception is that executive compensation is driven by greed.

THE DECLINE OF TRUST

It is probably no accident that criticism of executive compensation is rising at the same time as leader approval ratings are declining. Lucrative executive pay packages fly in the face of the great human value of fairness.[3] Should executives be rewarded for decisions that create hardship for their employees? Is it fair that the major automotive companies should resist restrictions on contracting out at the same time as they are earning record profits? Many people think it is morally irresponsible for an executive to accept rewards for actions of which their employees bear the brunt. As long as people perceive themselves as having to make do with small increases, they will be disturbed by executive practices that seem to be based on "unfair" criteria, especially when it involves levels of income quite outside their own

---

[2] "Unimpeachable Executive Pay," by Jude Rich, *American Compensation Association Journal*, 1995.

[3] See Chapter 5 for a full discussion of this unique aspect of our cultural identity.

experience. This approach has introduced a whole new set of considerations in compensation decision making.

The Sobeco Ernst & Young study showed that CEO base salary increases were 11 percent compared to just over 7 percent for division heads. At about the same time, the *Financial Post* leapt into the debate with several editorials challenging CEO compensation increases that failed to have corresponding increases in corporate performance. Widespread reporting of "poison pill" arrangements over the past few years has raised suspicions about the motives of some senior executives. According to Barry Cook, a partner with Western Management Consultants, companies and boards of directors are being challenged to assert, "We have not misspent your money." He points out that, whether executives like it or not, this intense interest in their pay and how it's determined is rapidly spreading beyond shareholders to clients, customers, the media and employees. "When you look at the combination of responsibilities and skills associated with the job," he adds, "I don't think the typical executive is overpaid."[4]

In many not-for-profit organizations, the CEO compensation package is determined by the board (usually by a committee on behalf of the board). Often the CEO compensation package is decided in a manner quite separate from the organization's official compensation program, the one that dictates the compensation of all other employees. With media increasing its reports and commentary on these and other aspects of executive compensation, no wonder public discomfort is rising!

THE PROS AND CONS OF VARIABLE INCOME SCHEMES

The widespread use of variable income—bonuses, commissions and stock options—is at the heart of the controversy. Variable income also goes by the names of incentive compensation, contingent pay and rewards management. Never before has variable compensation been applied as widely as it is today. Even as early as 1994, a study by the Conference Board indicated that 74 percent of organizations surveyed reported greater emphasis on variable pay. But that survey also revealed that variable pay was used for the more senior positions (76 percent for executives versus 41 percent for non-management).

There is a long-standing controversy over whether or not variable income makes sense as a concept. Alfie Kohn is one of the critics of incentive compensation.[5] He contends that incentive plans fail because they rest on incorrect

---

[4] As quoted in an article by Paul Luke entitled "Bosses Face Grilling Over Compensation," *Vancouver Province*, April 25, 1994.

psychological assumptions, arguing that incentives fail to create an enduring commitment to any value or action. Instead, they produce merely temporary compliance and, as such, are really bribes.

My own experience is that incentive compensation can work well. The relationship between business performance and incentive compensation is demonstrable in many companies, which makes variable income a perfectly legitimate strategic tool. There are, however, some risks and potential downsides that must be weighed and carefully monitored. If you provide a strong incentive for specified results, you are very likely to achieve them. But at what cost? Strong sales incentives, for example, may spur sales performance at the expense of gross margin or profit, or even customer service.

The issue is not whether incentive pay works, it is whether it works too well. Most incentive plans are based on individual performance objectives when organizations are emphasizing the importance of internal teamwork and collaboration more than ever. The fact is that some individual incentive plans may actually impede the development of cooperation with other individuals or organization units.

A similar problem arises from the tendency to base incentive compensation programs on short-term performance that may or may not be consistent with the long-term goals and strategies of the organization. This is a phenomenon which most experienced managers and executives understand well but seem powerless to address.

Designing effective variable income and incentive plans is difficult. The amount of time and energy required to adjust the plans can be prohibitively expensive. For example, how do the payout formulas deal with windfalls or catastrophes in cases where the actual performance differs from the expected by such a huge degree that the incentive plan will over- or under-reward? Senior management often succumbs to the temptation to apply common sense in such cases, adjusting the formula or performance indicators accordingly, in order to be fair to the participants. This demonstrates that management is prepared to intervene in a way which reduces the extent to which the compensation is at risk. And, without risk, it is difficult to see how there can be much incentive.

---

[5] "Why Incentive Plans Cannot Work," by Alfie Kohn, *Harvard Business Review,* Sept/Oct. 1993.

COMPENSATION DISTANCE

A closely related area of controversy is the compensation distance between the Chief Executive Officer and the other senior members of an executive group. At lower levels of the organization, the problem may be the opposite. The term "compression" describes a common problem, that of retaining enough distinction between supervisors and the people they supervise to make it worthwhile for them to accept supervisory or management responsibility. We have few benchmarks on compensation distance, just a few rules of thumb. But does it make sense for a CEO to make twice or more than other senior executives in an environment where decisions are normally made by consensus within senior management groups? Are CEOs any more accountable for the results? Do they take any greater personal risk? These are sensitive questions, since many boards and senior managers take the view that executive compensation is nobody else's business. The last thing we want to do it to remove incentive from organizational life so that it is no longer worthwhile to accept positions of increasing responsibility.

GREATER FLEXIBILITY

We must also bear in mind that these problems with executive compensation are occurring at a time of real innovation and positive change in compensation generally. There is a strong trend underway to move from the rigid, more bureaucratic forms of job evaluation towards more flexible compensation plans.

These innovations have led to sweeping modifications of traditional job evaluation in which the approach has been to measure the worth of a job regardless of who is doing it. This concept is gradually being replaced by pay for knowledge or skill programs which attempt to measure the value of the incumbent's competency.

The trend toward "broad-banding" is another important innovation. It reduces the need to make very fine, sometimes impossible, distinctions regarding the relative value of tasks and functions.

The concept of the "job rate" allows companies to pay rewards for veteran employees in the form of lump sum merit payments, rather than distorting their long-term compensation by continuing to reward exceptional performance which may have been limited to a few years.

All of these changes reflect new, positive and more flexible systems of rewarding human talent.

It is so easy to lose perspective in the field of compensation. I can recall so many debates within management committees over differences of less than one percent in the salary increase budget, and employees who complained bitterly about receiving salary increases a few dollars less than co-workers. To-the-death struggles between companies and their unions over cents per hour have become so common that we regard them as normal. Anyone accustomed to highly-variable income, with its periods of relative feast and famine, would find such compulsiveness about the size of a salary increase or the prospect of a compensation freeze bizarre.

Executive compensation may continue to attract greater public attention, or interest may fade. Regardless, it is in the interests of organizations to manage executive compensation carefully, in full expectation that the trend to greater disclosure will continue to gain force.

GUIDELINES FOR EXECUTIVE COMPENSATION

1. Eliminate the conflict of interest from the management of executive pay.

One way is to delegate executive compensation matters to a special committee of the board, often a compensation or human resource committee. In not-for-profit organizations this role can be played by the executive committee of the board. These committees should make sure that they obtain their own objective information and independent advice. It is acceptable to ask senior resource staff for their input, but not to rely solely on internal advice.

Sibson & Company's strategy to help boards create "unimpeachable" executive compensation includes a strong role for a board compensation committee: "to establish compensation principles, set performance goals, and ensure pay/performance alignment. Committee members should be independent, which requires that they do not serve on interlocking boards or compensation committees with the company CEO. Nor should committee members give significant services for profit to the company." [6]

But a board committee alone does not guarantee good and unbiased management of executive compensation. It must act on the basis of a sound framework of compensation policy and principle. Such a framework is as important for executive compensation as it is for other employees. One board negotiated a long-term compensation package for the CEO, including salary increases, when the industry was in the midst of restructuring. Everyone was painfully aware that the survival of the organization was in doubt. All other employees were in the third year of a salary freeze. If the board had been

---

[6] "Unimpeachable Executive Pay" by Jude Rich, *American Compensation Association Journal*, 1995.

working within the framework of an established compensation policy, developed for the whole organization, this rather serious discontinuity may not have occurred. A sound policy would clarify a target differential between CEO compensation and the other senior executives.

2. **Make a significant proportion of executive compensation contingent on performance.**

It is normal for executive compensation packages to contain a significant variable income component based on performance. Few people question the principle that leaders should be rewarded for performance; the question is how to put it into practice. Some executive reward schemes are based on the market price of the company's shares, but there can be a gap between share price and the underlying profit and return on investment performance. If the CEO compensation plan includes stock options, it may happen that the executive chooses to exercise the options during a period when corporate performance is less than stellar which, again, creates a discontinuity, or at least the *appearance* of a gap between the performance and the reward.

In not-for-profit organizations, particularly those that are publicly funded, meaningful variable income programs can be difficult to develop. Does it makes sense to reward an executive for spending less money than was budgeted? How do you measure growth of a publicly funded organization? Are the key economic decisions made by the CEO or the board? As demonstrated by the aftermath of the public disclosure of executive compensation in Ontario's public sector, clients and stakeholders of not-for-profits can be unsupportive of practices that are accepted as standard in the private sector.

The most important factor in the design and management of variable income plans for executives is how closely the organization's achievements relate to the rewards of its executives. "Nice try" management should be eliminated as a consideration in variable income. The essence of variable income is that it rewards exceptional results, not the quality of the effort. The admittedly understandable tendency of boards and senior managers to be fair may lead them to superimpose their judgment on the incentive formula and pay part of the reward, even if the targets were not achieved. They don't realize how seriously this undermines the fundamental incentive proposition. If people enjoy the rewards even when failing to achieve the desired outcomes, they come to realize that the compensation is not truly at risk. If it is not at risk, then it will not, in itself, provide incentive. The challenge for executive compensation administrators is to let the chips fall where they may on the variable income component of the package, even when non-controllable factors affect results significantly.

3. Balance short-term and long-term incentives.

As difficult as it is to establish valid measures of long-term performance, they play a vital role in any variable income program. By and large, organizations will get precisely the behavior for which they provide rewards. The principal responsibility of senior managers, particularly CEOs, is to shape the organization's future prosperity. If that goal is not reinforced in their compensation plan and if too much money is paid for short-term performance, they will drive the perspective of the management team away from the future and into the present.

Designing effective long-term incentive plans is probably the toughest technical problem in this highly technical field. What is the best measure of long-term performance? Is it year-to-year growth in pre-tax profit? Or is it some measure of shareholder value, such as return on investment or return on capital employed? The simplest approach in a publicly traded company is the market value of the company's shares, even though share price is subject to market fluctuations rather than corporate performance factors. Stock options, the most popular long-term incentive plan, have contributed to some of the controversy over executive pay. The rationale for high executive compensation based on exercising stock options is almost impossible to explain, in years when corporate performance is disappointing.

Organizations whose shares are not publicly traded must rely on other measures of long-term performance. Unfortunately, the validity of some of the resulting formulas are highly suspect. For example, phantom stock option plans set up a notional share value, based on profit or return on investment criteria, and pay long-term incentives accordingly.

Regardless of the mechanism selected, opportunities exist to achieve a close alignment between the organization's strategy and its long-term incentive plan, especially in organizations which have developed a quantifiable future vision, including such considerations as sales growth, and balance sheet factors such as return on assets and equity. In a cash-based long-term incentive plan, payouts can be tied directly to whether or not targeted levels of growth are achieved. It is also possible to include more qualitative forms, such as share of market, growth rate and so on. Some companies include the result of customer satisfaction surveys in the formula. Long-term incentives can be integrated with short-term incentives within the same variable income plans by including both a short- and long-term component. One problem, however, is that cash-based long-term incentive plans tend to be significantly more expensive, because unlike stock options, they require a cash outlay.

The search for the perfect long-term incentive formula will continue to consume compensation consultants, executives and boards, and this is good. The people at the top of organizations deserve to be rewarded for their success at shaping and positioning the organization for a successful future, especially when the pressure to focus on immediate problems is almost irresistible.

Barry Cook recommends that companies communicate to workers their executive's duties, how they are rewarded for meeting performance targets and how much the competition pays *its* bosses. Unless this is explained to them, employees may not realize that a particular bonus payment, for example, is related to the company performance six months to two years previously. Convincing employees that long-term incentive payouts are in the organization's best interest is a tall order. But Cook may be correct that it is an effort worth making.

4. Increase emphasis on organization-wide and team performance.

Senior executives, including CEOs, perform several roles in contemporary organizational life. Most function in at least three ways. First, as leaders of their part of the organization; second, as members of teams (such as management committees); and third, as individual contributors, as in the case of a vice president of marketing who makes a direct marketing contribution when he or she visits customers. Most decisions in today's organizations are made in a group setting where accountability for the results is shared by all who participate. We like to believe that the Chief Executive Office is the place where the "buck stops." But the reality is that most chief executives are in the position of endorsing decisions made by others. When an organization is committed to significant delegation of decision-making authority, the role of senior executives becomes increasingly to support and facilitate effective decisions. Organizations are highly individualistic in terms of how things actually happen and who is really involved in the full range of strategic and operational decisions. Executive compensation plans should be designed to reflect the real mix of individual and shared accountability.

Profit sharing and productivity gain sharing offer simple ways to reward people for organization-wide, rather than individual, performance. Perhaps the most frequent criticism leveled at profit sharing is that participants tend to be unaware of any strong link between their actions and the ultimate profit sharing pay-out. Still, profit sharing can provide people in private sector organizations with a real sense of ownership.

Productivity gain sharing suits some applications, particularly manufacturing settings, but is not well suited to every organization. Its most significant advantages lie in its ability to clarify goals and directions and to provide rewards for everyone's contribution. The main challenge in both profit sharing and productivity gain sharing is to develop a formula which people regard as fair. Profit performance of almost any company in almost any year will depend, to some degree, on external economic or competitive factors which are outside the influence of most employees. This sense that the outcome is beyond one's control tends to undermine the motivational power of these schemes. For an executive team, however, variable income based on corporate performance is often the simplest, most direct way of reinforcing the importance of team performance and the reality of shared accountability.

Individual rewards also have a place within an executive compensation package. Most of us recognize that our contribution to organizational success is partly individual and partly collective. We need affirmation that our unique and distinctive skills and accomplishments are recognized and valued. Executive compensation can acknowledge both team play and individual contributions.

Designing a meaningful individual component of compensation is straightforward in cases where performance can be readily evaluated through objective criteria. But in cases where a person's contribution is more difficult to assess objectively, it may be more practical to set up the individual components so that the scheme rewards specific, pre-determined accomplishments. So, for example, a dollar value could be easily attached to special achievements, such as the introduction of a new program, the successful completion of an important project, the introduction of a revised organization structure and so on.

When executive compensation can be designed both to recognize the individual and shared components of executive roles, this will help address the problems by aligning financial rewards and organization success. It sends out a clear message that good results come from everyone's efforts, not just the CEO's. The best response to critics of executive compensation practices is the ability to point to positive performance. Explaining how executive compensation reflects the teamwork that produced the result will further strengthen the argument.

5. **Manage executive compensation within established principles.**

Part of the problem behind the public's negative attitude towards executive compensation is that people generally don't understand it. They have been truly surprised by some of the figures reported. The compensation of Frank Stronach, Magna's Chairman, was down last year to $20.4 million from $47.2 million in the preceding year. Though this was apparently the result of the timing of exercising stock options, we are still talking about $47.2 *million*. It's naive to imagine that the public could be educated into acceptance of figures that high. A campaign to raise public support for executive compensation practices is hardly practical. What *does* seem to be relevant is that organizations be able, if asked, to explain the basic principles they apply to compensation matters in general and to executive compensation in particular, in order to reassure the public that their compensation practices are consistent and principled. The fact that it may indeed be none of anyone's business what an individual company decides to pay its president does not change the importance of basing an organization's practices on sound principles.

A tentative list of executive compensation principles should include:

- The compensation of everyone in the organization (including the president) will be managed within the organization's compensation policies and values.
- Pay for performance is a desirable principle and will be a feature of compensation plans where possible.
- Variable income payouts will reflect actual performance and not effort.
- Compensation rewards will balance short- and long-term considerations.
- The organization will be able to demonstrate that there has been no conflict of interest in compensation for senior executives.

It is not clear to what extent the growing influence of militant shareholder advocacy will force closer linkage of executive incentive pay and performance. But the linkage between executive compensation and leadership credibility is crystal clear. The same principles apply to them both—openness, fairness and equity. In their roles as customers, consumers and even employees, people feel entitled to an opinion about what senior executives are worth. Organizations need to hear these signals and manage compensation in full knowledge that previously private decisions will be the subject of public scrutiny. This can only be good, for public opinion provides an excellent test of the efficacy of such decisions.

CHAPTER **14**

THIS IS NOT A CONCLUSION

Sense: practical wisdom, judgment, common sense, conformity to these
Dignity: worth, nobleness, excellence
—from the *Oxford Illustrated Dictionary*, Oxford University Press 1962

The thorny issues raised in this book are familiar to anyone working within organizations. Unfortunately, there are no easy answers. As stressed in Chapter 1, while the ideas presented in *Coming to Our Senses* are intended to be thought-provoking and helpful, they are not highly prescriptive. They point at directions and not specific do's and don'ts. The book does not have a conclusion, for the conclusion rests in the hands of its readers.

You will bring your own wisdom and experience to bear on how you choose to deal with the challenges facing your organization. I hope that *Coming to Our Senses* succeeds in pointing you in some useful directions, and proves useful as a guide to the questions to be addressed when seeking solutions, but I do not presume to have the answers that will work for your organization in its particular situation. That is, of course, your business.

One of the great pleasures of working within organizations is that they are never entirely predictable and they are certainly never static. This makes the job of leadership endlessly challenging and always fascinating. It is up to each and every one of us to do what we can to improve the quality of the working experience within our organizations. In so doing, we will have contributed to building better and more efficient organizations. That is where the dignity lies —strong leadership depends on the ability to trust in your own practical wisdom, sound judgment and good common sense. That's the requirement.

I hope you will find these reflections helpful in developing your own "conclusion."